WITHDRAWN

THE MAKING

SS

THE MAKING OF BRITAIN

Echoes of Greatness

edited by
Lesley M. Smith

A CHANNEL
FOUR BOOK

MACMILLAN

First published 1988

Published by
MACMILLAN EDUCATION LTD
Houndmills, Basingstoke, Hampshire RG21 2XS
and London
Companies and representatives
throughout the world

Printed in Great Britain by
Richard Clay Ltd,
Chichester, Sussex

Typeset and designed by Columns of Reading

British Library Cataloguing in Publication Data
Echoes of Greatness.—(The Making of Britain)
1. Great Britain—History—20th century
I. Smith, Lesley M.   II. Series
941.082   DA566
ISBN 0–333–45654–8
ISBN 0–333–45655–6 Pbk

Contents

List of Illustrations

Acknowledgements

The publishers wish to acknowledge the following illustration sources:

The National Trust; Colorific Photo Library Ltd; BBC Enterprises Ltd; Gladstone Pottery Museum; Granada Television; John Frost Historical Newspapers; Popperfoto; Archiv Gerstenberg; BBC Hulton Picture Library; Imperial War Museum; Broadlands Archive; British Motor Industry Heritage Trust; Coventry City Libraries; Bede Gallery; Sheffield City Council; Greenwich Local History Library; Manchester Local History Library; The Keystone collection; Mansell Collection; Leeds City Libraries; First Garden City Heritage Museum; Camera Press Ltd; Bolton Museum and Art Gallery; The British Library; London Transport Museum; Dr Pat Thane; Rowntree plc; The Radio Times; Fabian Society; Wigan Record Office; The Photosource; National Gallery of Canada; National Museums and Galleries on Merseyside; Conservative Research Department; Mary Evans Picture Library; The Kobal Collection; Mike Laye, Daniel Day Lewis and Gordon Warnecke Press Association Ltd.

Every effort has been made to trace all the copyright holders but if any have been inadvertently overlooked the publishers will be pleased to make the necessary arrangement at the first opportunity.

Preface

This book accompanies the fifth and final series of LWT/Channel Four's survey of British history, *The Making of Britain*. I should like to thank all those at London Weekend Television who have been involved with this series: Barry Cox, Jane Hewland, Robin Paxton, whose comments did much to shape the final version of both the series and the book, and Johanna Pool. All the contributors to the book have generously shared with me their knowledge of the twentieth century and brought to our project an enthusiasm which has made this series particularly enjoyable. A number of other scholars have also spent time discussing the twentieth century with me and I should like to thank particularly David Anderson, Linda Colley, Leonore Davidoff, Christopher Harvie, Paul Johnson, Jane Lewis, Sara Maitland, Robert Pearce, and Lavinia Warner. Linda Stradling accomplished the very extensive picture research for both the book and the series with patience and skill. Her efficiency and good humour also helped to keep the project running smoothly over the last months of preparation. I am also grateful to Pam Wilkinson who again typed the manuscript for me. Finally, throughout the five years we have worked on *The Making of Britain*, Pat Newbert, our Unit Manager in the Features department, and her secretary, Marcelle Ruddell, have done everything they could to solve any problems that arose. In thanks, I should like to dedicate this book to them.

LMS

Introduction

Lesley M. Smith

Facing the birth of the twentieth century, Chekhov wrote in his notebook:

> we struggle to change life so that those who come after us might be happy, but those who come after us will say as usual; it was better before, life is now worse than it used to be.

With only twelve years of this century left before a new millenium, we can say with confidence that no society has dabbled so thoroughly in nostalgia as Britain over the last fifty years. Certainly the last two decades have echoed with the voices of reaction. But there is more afoot than a simple nostalgia for past glories. Our attitude to the recent past reflects deep changes in our interpretation of what is good or bad in modern society.

The idea that the past was better than the present would have shocked all but a minority in nineteenth-century Britain. Then everyone in Britain had to come to terms with the fact that industrialisation had changed traditional ways of life based on agriculture and the land, and was likely to continue doing so. The control and regulation of change became the *raison d'être* of governments. In the long run, change constituted progress, and progress would ultimately benefit all. Most people in Britain today still believe this. But progress in the 1980s bears little relation to the arcadian vision of the Victorians.

At the beginning of the First World War, simply to be free from hunger was a luxury for many working people. But once hunger was conquered, and survival assured, people had the luxury to think about status. Was one middle class or working class? Was the family respectable or not? Material possessions were the key. Respectability among the working and middle classes was displayed in pianos and looking-glasses, or by wearing the appropriate clothes for weddings and funerals. Retaining a full-time servant or keeping the children well-shod was a vital signal in the social game.

Not only did individuals aspire to better themselves, they did so within an atmosphere inherited from the nineteenth-century reformers that assumed comfortable, middle-class life was the ultimate goal for everyone. Anyone interested in changing society for the better did so with this aim in mind, whether they justified it by the application of socialist principles or through the fear of revolution in the streets. And continue to change the world they did. Beating hunger and the worst effects of poverty was only the first hurdle.

Even before the First World War, new goals headed the reformers' agenda. It was now not simply enough to ensure that everyone had a home. Each family had to have a good home. More children at the beginning of the twentieth century survived into adulthood than ever before. But now survival in itself was not enough; they had to enjoy good health and as long a life as medical science could provide. Individual reformers such as Seebohm Rowntree, civil servants and even government ministers poured their effort into satisfying these goals. And between the 1930s and the 1950s, something like the clean, healthy, respectable world they imagined came into existence.

Slumdwellers are still being rehoused in the 1980s. But slum clearance or the provision of some education to all children no longer provides the emotive issue at elections, swinging voters between one party and the other. Post-war Britain was, and still is, sufficiently wealthy to provide the basic requirements of life – homes, jobs, schooling to the middle teens, higher education, support in times of hardship – to almost every citizen from birth to death. With the satisfaction of our practical needs assured, albeit for several million people by state subsidy, our ideas of progress have shifted to encompass more intangible influences on the quality of life.

When people in the 1930s moved from overcrowded slums to three-bedroomed houses with hot and cold running water whether or not they were happy in their new homes was not an issue. If anything, local authorities and successive governments assumed that good physical conditions *guaranteed* contentment, if not exuberant delight. Where the government's aim in the 1930s was to feed the families of the unemployed, it plans, in the 1980s, to restore self-confidence and a sense of purpose, by training and Jobstart programmes for the cooperative and loss of benefits for the intransigent. Now, the lack of job satisfaction, self-respect, of security, neighbourliness, good relationships – some, if not all, the components of a reasonably happy co-existence with society – are seen to be the problems we need to tackle in the name of progress. Yet with so many material needs met for the majority in Britain, where do we look for our solutions?

The first solution is more of what we have already in abundance: more houses, more cars, more holidays, more owner-occupiers, more shareholders. The second suggests that as all the external benefits of twentieth-century life, more often legislated for and organised by the state, if not always financed by it, have failed to convince us that life is better now than once it was, perhaps the last recourse is to look within ourselves for the solutions to society's problems.

Thus we have experienced over the last thirty years a flourishing consumerism linked with an ever-deepening scrutiny of the individual. Britain is not alone in following this progression. Western society as a whole sometimes resembles a fractious child. When all its wants have been met, it then announces that the problem was actually something quite different. The struggle for survival has given way to the search for self-fulfilment.

Some of the side-effects are obviously beneficial. Individuals have greater confidence in their own judgements: the idea of self-help has spread into almost every human activity. Individuals can exert greater control over their own lives, and exercise choice at many more stages in their lives. But other effects are less pleasant: a lack of interest in the fate of fellow citizens outwith our own immediate ambit, and an intuition that it is only successful individuals who can create a successful society.

At the beginning of the twentieth century, the state took on new responsibilities in changing society for the better. Only the future will tell whether this massive accretion of responsibilities is more than a short-term response to a particular set of social and political problems. But already, in the 1980s, we judge inadequate the 'progress' orchestrated by the state. Now the onus is falling once more on the individual, just as it has done for much of human history.

This evolution in our interpretation of progress forms the background to the twelve chapters in this volume. The book is not an encyclopaedic history of Britain in the twentieth century. But we have tried to look at events or areas of everyday life where the nature of change illuminates the experiences of people living in Britain today and perhaps offers us a more accurate perspective on the present than the nostalgia to which Chekhov condemned each new generation.

The source of our nostalgia is the belief that Britain is sunk deep into irrevocable decline. Nowhere has this infused our thinking more than in the field of international relations. The massive presence of John Bull around the globe has been transformed into the insignificant terrier, yapping alternately at the heels of America and the European Economic Community. In his chapter, David Reynolds argues that all the Western European nations have declined in that they have lost in the twentieth century the empires that enabled them to dominate the nineteenth. Empire is still the key to international success, but it is the territorially coherent and richly resourced empires of America and Russia that today call the international tune.

Despite this, Britain has twice triumphed in world wars, only to find the price of victory greater than other nations found the cost of defeat, while the fact that relations within the empire remained relatively amicable after the Second World War shielded Britain for many years from the necessity of coming to terms with the changing conditions for world power. Britain has had a more difficult adjustment than most to the realities of twentieth-century global politics not simply because the nation had so much to lose but also because for much of the century it exploited its remaining strengths more successfully than any other European nation.

Another area where notions of decline are deeply entrenched is the economy. Deserted mines and abandoned factories are the images that express Britain's economic performance in the 1980s. But Richard Overy argues that the images lie. The economy has grown steadily throughout the century, and by investigating the economic realities that lie behind the statistics supporting his claims, he demonstrates that the same problems we face today have been an integral, but not insuperable, factor throughout the last hundred years. The familiar North-South divide, for example, is as old as the last decades of the nineteenth century, when the special problems of industrial obsolescence were first recognised. Although the successive waves of re-industrialisation – cars, bicycles and domestic consumer goods in the middle decades of the twentieth century, electronics and service industries in the 1980s – have widened that divide, they have also more than sustained Britain's continued economic prosperity and our own standards of living.

Leslie Hannah's chapter echoes these findings, although he approaches the problem from a different perspective. Even those who face the loss of jobs or contemplate a world in which their skills are no longer relevant are much more prosperous than they would have been at any other point in the twentieth century. He reveals that our perceptions of decline are directly contradicted by our own experiences of ever-increasing personal prosperity. Moreover, it is not the redistribution of wealth within Britain that has so boosted our personal income, but the ability of our much-maligned economy to generate new sources of wealth and income. Partly conditioned by comparisons with other countries, we are dissatisfied with our economy not because it does not fulfil our expectations, but because it does not do so fast enough. In the shortfall between reality and aspirations lie the origins of our belief in Britain's economic weakness.

Our expectations of life in modern society are much more complex than they were at the end of the nineteenth century. For much of the century, faith in modernity has simplified the agenda for Utopia. Nowhere has this been more apparent than in the physical environment in which we live. John Stevenson traces the rise and fall of the conviction that ordered, planned, modern surroundings for work, home and leisure would quickly abolish all social problems. The prosperity of the 1950s and 1960s, combined with the damage left by the war, presented a *carte blanche* on which the New Jerusalem could be built. The transformation brought tower blocks, shopping centres and ring-roads to Britain, but proved no more therapeutic an environment than the one it replaced.

One area where change did occur through individual effort is that relating to women's place within society. Pat Thane discards the belief that women's aspirations throughout the century have been consistent, and explores the ambiguities of women's struggle for equality in the modern world. Liberation meant different things at different times in the century, and to different classes. Leisured middle-class women wanted the social freedom to take an active part in professional and political life, enjoying a rich life outwith the home. Many poor women, struggling both to work and to raise children, longed for the economic freedom to abandon work and concentrate fully on domestic life. The changing role of women is not a simple linear progression towards equality with men. Instead, through a combination of pragmatism and courage, women have won a wider choice in planning their own futures than ever before.

Much of our freedom of choice comes from our awareness of alternatives to our own lives and aspirations. At the end of the nineteenth century, people were bound by what they could see and hear within their own communities for information about the outside world. Paddy Scannell investigates the way radio and television brought the world, whether it be Westminster or Wisconsin, into the home. The mass media democratised Britain, bringing not only classical music and theatre to ordinary people, but legitimising their struggles and way of life as subjects for plays, documentaries and serials. But in tandem with culture, radio brought an enhanced awareness of politics to the voters enfranchised after the First World War. News and comments from the wider world provided for millions of people the education that enabled them to make an informed use of their new political rights.

Many of those people chose to vote for a party newly prominent at Westminster and in the constituencies, the Labour Party. Kenneth Morgan investigates the rise of working-class politics, from the first fragmented groups claiming to represent workingmen's interests to the triumphant party that took power in 1945 with a programme of socialist reform dedicated to the eradication of poverty and inequality in Britain. Indeed, the recent electoral failures of the Labour Party have their source within that success. For so thorough was the work of the Labour Party in changing the political agenda of *all* parties in Britain that the ideals of workers' solidarity and socialism are no longer relevant to the majority of the party's traditional constituency.

Ben Pimlott investigates a different aspect of our recent political history, stressing that our understanding of the past can be distorted by the political needs of the present. Political leaders and journalists now characterise the middle decades of the twentieth century as a time of consensus, when all the major parties agreed on the main lines of government policy. This underlines the sharp conflicts apparent today and accentuates in ways attractive to politicians on the right and on the left their separate and radical remedies for the future. But he argues that the evidence of the day suggests from the 1940s on a politics just as bitter and confrontational as it is today. Consensus might be a useful propaganda weapon for politicians but it belongs in the capacious records devoted to historical myth.

Another such myth shrouds the origins of the modern welfare state in clouds of pure idealism and self-sacrifice. Adrian Wooldridge shows that the founders of the welfare state were much more interested in building a healthy population into invincible armies to protect the empire than in improving the health and welfare of the poor as a general social good. Throughout the first half of the century, welfare legislation provided no more than a safety net in times of extreme need. Only during the prosperous 1960s was there sufficient cash to allow governments to use the welfare state as an instrument of social engineering, promoting greater equality within Britain in a way that would have horrified both Beveridge and his predecessors.

The vibrant manufacturing economy of post-war Britain brought other social changes. With a labour shortage at home, the government invited West Indian citizens to work in Britain. Michael Gilkes looks at the history of both Britain and the Caribbean to explain why these new arrivals, who shared a common culture and a single language with Britain, should have proved the most successful of the many waves of migrants who contributed to the Britain we know today. Yet within ten years of the first mass arrivals, the Notting Hill riots of 1958 demonstrated just how much racial violence lay beneath the surface of everyday life. The ineptitude of successive governments in promoting a genuine multi-racial society has ensured that each generation of black men and women has had to come to terms anew with the reality of living in a society still only half-reconciled to their presence.

David Cannadine and Michael Ignatieff both ponder the wider role of history itself within British society today. Each generation re-interprets the past as a reflection of its own experiences, so that Britain has not one history but many, each illuminating a fragment of the present as well as a chapter of the past. Yet David Cannadine warns that we are in danger of losing all contact with that past. While interest in country houses, conservation of the physical remains of the past, and local or family history has never been greater, the only framework capable of making sense of these historical impressions, the history of Britain itself, is neglected or abandoned to academic circles alone.

Without an understanding of the past, we risk also losing control of the future. Britain is at a crossroads, and developments over the next decades may radically change the nation we know today. Michael Ignatieff shows how the growing economic and cultural inter-nationalism of the late twentieth century will determine how we in Britain will live. Despite pressing problems such as the relationship between the Third World and western society, or the destructive capacity of the major powers, he discovers within British society a shared sense of purpose that may yet sweep us unscathed into the twenty-first century.

Anyone trying to understand the twentieth century faces the burden of too much reality. We have generated the raw material of history in unprecedented quantities: pamphlets, magazines, newspapers, govern-ment papers, diaries, letters, and books threaten to swamp every archive and library. Then there are the new sources of information about the past. Voice recordings, films, newsreels, television and satellite put sound and vision to history as it happens. Yet without objective judgements about the world in which we live it is almost impossible to go behind the violence of newspaper debate and the conflicting claims of politicians to distinguish rhetoric from reality. If we stop trying to understand what happened in the 1950s, the 1960s, or even the 1970s, our ability to imagine the future, much less shape it, collapses.

The Past in the Present

David Cannadine

There is more to the history of modern Britain than the account of what has happened to our country during the twentieth century. And there is more to the writing of history than the production of a definitive version of the national past. For countries, like people, do not just make their history, once and for all, as and when it actually happens. They also remake it, again and again, after the event. To this extent all people, and all nations, live in the past as well as in the present. And modern Britain is no exception to this general rule. As a result, we cannot understand the history of our country in the twentieth century, unless we also understand how modern Britain has made sense of the centuries that have gone before.

No society in human history has ever been completely free of its past. At a very basic level, most of us want to know where we have come from, and what things were like before we were born. But the past can also be made to serve other purposes. Suitably presented, it can legitimate authority in one guise, or justify revolution in another. Depending on the needs of the present, it can be used to provide inspiration and reassurance, or escapism and nostalgia. Even the professional historians disagree as to what they should study, and how they should study it. For while the past is over, dead and gone, the particular aspects of it which any generation of scholars chose to investigate are as much determined by their own contemporary circumstances as they are by the evidence which the past has left behind.

All of this is well shown by the changing ways in which the British have viewed their own national past during the last one hundred years or so. As subsequent chapters in this book will make plain, the twentieth century has been a crowded and tumultuous era, with dramatic changes in Britain's international standing and domestic circumstances. And this in turn has greatly influenced the ways in which we have looked at and made sense of our past – not only in terms of changing popular perceptions, but also in terms of shifting scholarly priorities. In the course of this essay, I want to investigate how our sense of the national past and of national history has changed during the last one hundred years.[1] But it is probably best to begin with a description of how we see Britain's past and Britain's history now, in the 1980s.

I

Beyond any doubt, our country today is in many ways quite besotted with its past. At the very apex of our government and society is the monarchy, and much of its appeal derives from its links with times long since vanished. The queen traces her ancestors back well over a thousand years, and this provides a comforting sense of continuity with the present. And much of the magic of the monarchy depends on its essentially anachronistic ceremonial, with its horses and carriages and picturesque uniforms.[2] In the same way, our politicians regularly and eagerly look to the past for inspiration. From one perspective, Mr Tony Benn summons up the Levellers when calling for more radical policies; while from another, Mrs Thatcher extols Victorian values, thereby appealing to the popular sense that the nineteenth century was our country's last – and greatest – golden age.[3]

1.1. Queen Elizabeth II riding in the state coach

1.2. Keith Mitchell as
Henry VIII

1.3. Glenda Jackson as
Elizabeth I of England

1.4. *Brideshead Revisited*

1.5. A National Trust craftsman restoring plaster work

Not surprisingly, the media are also obsessed with the past, both real and imagined. From Henry VIII and Queen Elizabeth I to Lloyd George and Winston Churchill, the great figures from our history have been recreated on our television screens, bringing into our own homes the most vivid image yet of our national past. Make-believe dramas, such as *The Forsytes*, *The Jewel in the Crown* and *Brideshead Revisited*, have been if anything even more popular with television audiences. A large sector of Britain's reading public is at least as historically minded. Best-selling biographies, of the great and the good, the infamous and the notorious, have always been, and still are, the salvation of many a despairing publisher's list. And the popular appetite for historical novels and romances is insatiable, as the sales of writers such as Dorothy Dunnett, Jean Plaidy, Catherine Cookson and Barbara Cartland serve to show.

But for many people in Britain today, history means one thing above all others: the national heritage. There have never been so many pressure groups so concerned with — and so successful at — preserving pieces of the national past as there are in the 1980s. When the owner of a stately home is obliged to sell some pictures, or when an old building is threatened with destruction, the conservationists emerge in full and ferocious cry. When the *Mary Rose* was raised, the nation watched and rejoiced. The National Trust is more popular than it has ever been; country houses and art galleries are crammed with visitors; and a new museum opens in Britain once every two weeks.[4] The industrial economy may be in terminal decline; but the heritage economy is unquestionably booming.

Many museums, like the Gladstone Pottery Museum at Stoke-on-Trent, are concerned to preserve the regional past, and seek to evoke the everyday lives of ordinary men and women in particular localities. Organisations such as the History Workshop movement and the Oral History Society are equally concerned to recover the past experience of those who are more often seen as the victims, rather than the makers, of history. In schools and at adult education classes, it is courses in local history, which explore the past on your own doorstep, which now have much the greatest appeal. And each year, thousands of people visit their local library and county record office, and look at old maps and census data in the search for their ancestors. Twenty years ago, it was only the Americans who wanted to find their roots here: today it seems as though everyone in Britain is doing so.

Seen from this perspective, fascination with the past has probably never been so intense or so widespread in Britain as it is today. Yet oddly enough, while popular interest in the past is great and growing, popular interest in our national history as a whole is dwindling and decaying. The monarchy and the media, the politicians and the

1.6. Princes Risborough, one of the National Trust properties

conservationists, the local historians and the ancestor worshippers, may be passionately involved with particular pieces of the past. But very few of them are concerned with the broader framework of national history and chronological sequence, which would give deeper and richer meaning to these local, personal and partial impressions. There may be a nostalgia boom in Britain today; but there is also an uncontrolled epidemic of national amnesia. We are so busy searching for our roots that we have lost our way in the garden.

Today in Britain, there are probably fewer people with an adequate, working knowledge of our country's history than at any previous time in the twentieth century. In many secondary schools, very little British history is taught at all, and over half of the pupils study no history whatsoever beyond the age of 15. At 'O' and at 'A' Level, and also therefore at university, the number of people studying history is declining alarmingly.[5] The result is plain for all to see. Most people — and especially young people — do not know whether St Paul's Cathedral is older than Westminster Abbey, whether the Tudors came before the Stuarts, or whether Marlborough is a duke or a cigarette. How can we make sense of Mr Benn's and Mrs Thatcher's historical allusions, if we are ignorant of the history to which they are alluding?

There may be interest in particular aspects of the national past, but fewer and fewer people have any overall sense of how these bits and pieces fit into a broader, chronological account of our country's history.

II

It has not always been like this. During the period from the 1870s to the 1930s, the picture was very different. The Education Act of 1870 meant that elementary schooling was at last available for almost the whole of the population, and the teaching of national history formed an integral part of the curriculum. At Oxford and Cambridge universities, the number of undergraduates studying the subject massively expanded, as history became the best possible training for the governing elite of the nation and the empire.[6] And the major figures in public life – Salisbury and Gladstone, Rosebery and Asquith, Curzon and Baldwin – possessed a powerful sense of the past, and all of them understood their own nation in essentially historical terms.

At all levels of society, the past in general, and the British past in particular, was thus an integral part of national life. But why exactly was this so? It is important to remember that the years from 1870 to 1940 witnessed the zenith of the European nation state. Before 1914, the majority of the world was effectively divided up between a handful of great powers, and during the inter-war years Europe itself witnessed a sustained experiment in the construction of new countries.

1.7. Exhibit of decorative sanitary ware, Gladstone Working Pottery Museum

Throughout this period, the nation state was seen as the focus of individual loyalty and as the mainspring of political action.[7] As such, it was countries, rather than individuals, which made history. And this veneration of the national state greatly stimulated the study of national history.

In Britain, as in most western countries, the history which was produced under these circumstances was of a particular kind. It provided a narrative account of what were deemed to be the most significant events in the national past, most of which were essentially political: war and peace, kings and queens, and the like. But in the British case, this added up to something special – a self-congratulatory account of how a small country avoided invasion and revolution, pioneered ordered progress and constitutional government, and so established itself as the greatest nation and the greatest empire in the world.[8] At one level, the very act of describing the British past shed light on a contemporary world where Britain seemed pre-eminent. At another, this chronological account of the national past provided an historical framework within which ordinary people made sense of their lives and their surroundings.

Of course, this period also witnessed the growth of many bodies such as the National Trust and the Survey of London, which were concerning themselves with what would now be called the national heritage. But in this earlier period, to a much greater extent than today, these conservationists saw themselves as working within the context of this broader framework established by national history. The *Victoria County Histories*, for instance, provided a chronological account of the evolution of the county community, which was itself envisaged as one of the major building blocks of the nation state. The *Dictionary of National Biography* was designed to celebrate all national worthies throughout our country's history.[9] And the countless biographies of politicians and statesmen took it for granted that great men made history by their work for the nation.

Whatever their specific historical concern, these people did not lose sight of the broader picture: they still thought of the past in essentially national terms. So did those many writers who were much preoccupied at this time with what was called the national character. Self-evidently, the very notion of a national character transcended the divisions of class and the boundaries of locality. But the national character was also an essentially historical construct, the cause and the consequence of the nation's past experience. While other nations lurched from revolution to disaster, the British people advanced in orderly manner along their pre-destined path to greatness. Moderation and decency were thus the essence of the national character, the theme of national history and the key to national success.[10]

All this emerged most memorably in that classic work of national history and national comedy written at the very end of this period: *1066 and All That*, by W.C. Sellar and R.J. Yeatman, first published in 1930. Significantly, both of these men were schoolteachers, and they drew on their professional experience to send up the prevailing notion of English history, with the gentlest of humour and the greatest of affection. For all the jokes, the puns and the howlers, the image of England's past which they present is instantly recognisable. It begins with Caesar's invasion of Britain, and proceeds via the Battle of Hastings to the Civil War. And it concludes with the War of 1914 to 1918, which was 'the cause of nowadays, and thus the end of history'. As usual, history is conceived of in essentially national, political and chronological terms. It is about kings and queens and great events. It is the story of Britain's rise to being top nation. And as such, it took for granted a detailed knowledge of national and narrative history.

III

Yet today in Britain, the majority of the population – from the professional historians downwards – do not understand more than a handful of the jokes in that book, and so neither know nor care whether the Spanish Armadillo was a better swimmer than the Great Seal. It is easy to see why: in a country simultaneously besotted with national nostalgia but blighted with national amnesia, they do not know the history which is the crucial precondition for appreciating the humour. But how do we explain this? Why is it that the years since the Second World War have seen both the decline of national history and also the rise of national heritage? Why have most people in Britain ceased to envisage the past – their past – in essentially national terms, and have come to think of it instead as a patchwork of disconnected fragments, local events and individual interests, without any broader frame of reference?

Part of the answer is that throughout the western world, which once so venerated the nation state (and the nation's history), our sense of national power has been much diminished. Since the Second World War, we have simply ceased to believe that the state is the mainspring of political action, the controller of human destiny. In so many ways, it now seems to be global forces, rather than national impulses, which shape our lives. Living as we do, in the shadows of environmental disaster, nuclear holocaust, international terrorism and epidemic catastrophe, the nation state seems powerless in the face of these global threats. And in western Europe, the erosion of national autonomy seems especially pronounced: most of the decisions affecting our future seem to be taken in Brussels or New York, in

Tokyo or Kuwait, but no longer within the national capitals themselves.

Put another way, this means that the nation states of the West no longer make history in the way that they once did – or were thought to have done. The decline and disappearance of the old European empires, the emancipation of the third world, and the rise of the superpowers, means that there is no longer anything intrinsically superior or uniquely significant about western nations, or about their history.[11] Indeed, since contemporary events are more influenced by what happens in America, Russia, China and the Middle East than by what goes on in Britain, Italy or Spain, those who seek a historical perspective on the present are probably better advised to study the world beyond Europe rather than the history of our own continent or of our own nation.

This decline in national self-esteem has been especially marked in the case of Britain itself, since by definition the top nation had the most to lose. Stripped of its empire and its great power status, our country no longer carries as much weight in the affairs of the world as it once did. Economically and politically, Britain is now, once again, a collection of small islands off the coast of Europe, uncertain whether its future lies across the Channel or across the Atlantic. Domestically, too, the country seems increasingly divided: between England and the Celtic fringe, between the North and the South, between blacks and whites, between the employed and the out-of-work.[12] Under these reduced circumstances, those comforting and essentially historical notions, of national identity, of national character, of national mission and of a national past, seem to most people at best outmoded and at worst plain irrelevant.

But these global developments since the Second World War have also influenced – and changed – the way professional historians have looked at the past. For just as they have led to a decline in popular interest in national history, so they have also led to the devaluation of national history as a scholarly endeavour. The most formidably destructive influence here has been that of the French historians known as the *Annales* school.[13] Since the late 1940s, they have asserted that it is the long-term changes, in the climate and the environment, in the economy and in social relations, which are the prime movers of history. The short-term political actions, of men and women, of nations and states, are relegated to a peripheral place in the historical drama, and to a subordinate position in the hierarchy of historical causation. Viewed in this light, the nation is not the mainspring of history at all: it is more the passive victim than the active initiator of events.

In the same way, the proliferation of history since the Second World

War into a variety of sub-specialisms has further accentuated this professional trend away from the study of the national past. Economic history, social history, urban history, women's history and black history – subjects which have seemed of the greatest contemporary relevance and concern – are rarely conceptualised or written about by professional scholars in national terms.[14] Once again, they are more concerned with the underlying forces such as class, capitalism, urbanisation, race and gender than with specifically national influences. The result is a version of the past in which blacks or women or workers or city dwellers have more in common with the same people in other countries than they have with different people in the same country. The idea that the nation is the prime unit of historical experience or historical explanation is not something with which these historians are much concerned.[15]

Ironically enough, many recent developments within political history – which once provided the broad chronological framework for understanding our country's past – have only reinforced this trend away from national history. Much of it has been so localised and parochial in its focus that the broader national perspectives have often been completely lost sight of. Some of it which does address national subjects covers such a small span of time that it gives little sense of chronology, except that very often it denies any major landmarks in our national past at all. The growth of interest in the poor and the protesting has often led historians to ignore the structure of power and authority which the state itself provided. Even biography has suffered a scholarly eclipse: it is no longer fashionable to believe that great men – let alone great women – make national history. And a great deal of the resulting scholarly output has been written in language so dense and impenetrable that it has ceased to appeal to the broader reading public, and has only been of interest to a small group of fellow-professionals.

So, the greatest irony of all in the Britain of the 1980s is that these developments in professional history have reinforced, rather than countered, the current popular obsession with a fragmented and piecemeal past. Most professional historians today are no longer the keepers of our corporate memory as a nation, and are failing to provide that broader national framework within which particular pieces of the past might be located. They, too, are more interested in experience than in narrative,[16] in one-off events than in chronology. They, too, often lack any real sense of time or place. And in this world in which our national standing and our national history have both suffered such attrition, is it any wonder that the British public are more concerned with the raising of the *Mary Rose* or the quest for their ancestors than with any more broadly-based conception of our national past?[17]

IV

So is there any future for history as the account of our national past? Clearly, the clock cannot – and should not – be put back to the world of *1066 and All That*. We cannot unlearn or ignore that mass of history published since 1945 which repudiates the view that the nation is the mainspring of all past human action. We must also accept that in our more crowded and complex world, where Britain plays a smaller part than it once did, it is vital to study the histories of other nations if we would wish to understand the present by looking at the past. And even if we do want to know about the British past, we must recognise that national identity, national autonomy and national character are no longer such compelling – or such historical – notions as they once were.

But there is another side to this. For in a country so obsessed with particular parts of the past, the need to provide a broad, national, chronological framework within which they might be set is clearly pressing and urgent. After all, the majority of British people still live their lives within the confines of this particular nation state, and it is surely right that they should have as much sense of its past as of its present. Above all, as one or two inspired practitioners of scholarly history have shown in the years since the Second World War, it is still possible to write histories of Britain which are accessible, appealing and even inspiring. Although it should no doubt be more modestly conceived than in the high noon of empire or the heyday of the nation state, we still need a national framework to make sense of our individual historical experience.[18]

Further Reading

D. Horne, *The Great Museum* (London, 1984); D. Lownethal, *The Past is a Foreign Country* (Cambridge, 1985); J.H. Plumb, *The Death of the Past* (London, 1969); W.C. Sellar and R.J. Yeatman, *1066 and All That* (Harmondsworth, 1965); L. Stone, *The Past and the Present* (London, 1981); P. Wright, *On Living in an Old Country* (London, 1985).

CHAPTER TWO

Britannia Overruled: the Shrinking of a World Power

David Reynolds

In 1870 Great Britain was the principal world power. It controlled roughly a fifth of the earth's surface, including India, Canada and Australasia. It was also the world's leading economy, accounting for nearly a quarter of total manufacturing output and a similar proportion of world trade. The first industrial nation had become the greatest empire in world history.

A century later Britain was no longer 'Great'. Shorn of nearly all its overseas possessions, it had shrunk into an off-shore European island – a rather sulky member of the European Community. Its manufacturing base had collapsed and it was almost on a par with Italy in per capita output and income. By 1979 the first post-industrial nation was struggling to find its post-imperial role.

Why did Britain's place in the world change so dramatically? Was it loss of nerve?[1] Or was it the consequence of a fossilised economic and social system?[2] Certainly internal explanations are important. But Britain's fate was not unique. It was part of a more general pattern – the disintegration of all the European empires and the eclipse of Europe by the superpowers, America and Russia. We also need to remember that Britain remained an important force in the world for much of this period, until the 1960s. In fact, it was not so much that Britain declined, but that others rose – like towering office blocks on the skyline of the City of London, overshadowing the once solitary grandeur of St Paul's. So our explanation has to take account of developments in the world at large, not merely in Britain itself.

Britain's supremacy was unintentional. It derived not from any clear-cut blueprint for global hegemony but from the need to protect Britain's worldwide commercial interests and to prevent hostile powers from extending their own possessions. But by the late Victorian period Britain's international dominance was clear, and it rested on three main foundations. First, Britain controlled the population and resources of much of the non-European world. Second, it maintained its global reach through command of the leading military technology of the day – seapower. Third, it was the world's principal industrial and financial nation. As the twentieth century progressed, however, these foundations were undermined. Colonies and clients proved increasingly resistant to imperial exploitation; developed states became more effective competitors, both military and economic. First, I want to look very generally at how these three foundations of British power collapsed – the imperial, the military and the economic. Then I shall examine the effect of the two world wars in accelerating that process.

First, Britain's changing imperial base. By themselves the British Isles were of limited potential. At the beginning of this century Russia had 133 million people, America 76 million and the United Kingdom only 42 million.[3] But add in the British Empire and the picture looked very different. At its peak in 1933 the empire covered nearly a quarter of the world's land surface and embraced nearly a quarter of its population, some 500 million in all.[4]

At the heart of the empire was India. Britain had no large conscript army of its own, unlike most of the continental powers. India provided the military manpower which, at little cost to the British taxpayer, could be deployed in support of imperial interests in a great arc from China to Egypt. In the First World War nearly 1.4 million troops from India were sent overseas to fight for their king emperor.[5] At this time India was also the largest single market for British goods, and its own exports – such as jute, cotton and rice – helped Britain balance its trade with the Continent and North America. In 1901 Lord Curzon predicted: 'As long as we rule India we are the greatest power in the world. If we lose it we shall drop straight away to a third rate power.'[6]

Yet the empire was something of a con trick. Britain lacked the resources to control others by brute force alone. Empire rested on a judicious balance of selective repression, collaboration with local leaders, and the satisfaction of key economic concerns such as food, prices and land tenure.[7] During the twentieth century that balancing act became less easy to sustain. As colonies and territories developed their own political systems, so they were better able to resist British demands. Often London conceded greater autonomy – especially to the 'White Dominions' of Canada, South Africa, Australia and New Zealand. Yet this meant less control over their economic resources, even though Britain still remained largely responsible for their defence. In non-white societies such as Egypt and India the British also made political concessions, but they often applied greater force to maintain their position. A notorious example was the Amritsar massacre of 1919 when British troops fired on Indian demonstrators and nearly 400 died.

Either way – concession or repression – the net costs of empire escalated. And repression proved at best a delaying action, as the government of India found when dealing with Gandhi and the Congress Party. In 1940, London agreed that henceforth India would pay only for the costs of its own defence. The use of Indian troops abroad was to be financed by Britain. By 1945 Britain owed India at least £1.3bn for services rendered during the war.[8] After renewed violence forced London to concede independence in 1947 the British were unable to draw on Indian manpower and resources at any price.

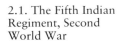

2.1. The Fifth Indian Regiment, Second World War

2.2. Mountbatten speaking during the Independence ceremonies, India, 1947

As Curzon had predicted, the loss of India was decisive for Britain's global power. But the pattern was repeated elsewhere. In the nineteenth century Britain struck out. In the twentieth century the empire struck back. Gradually Britain released or was forced to release its grip on the world's population and resources – first in the Indian subcontinent, then during the 1950s in the Middle East, finally and precipitously in Africa in the 1960s. By 1979 Queen Elizabeth II ruled only about as much of the world as her illustrious namesake had done four centuries before.

The loss of empire was thus an integral part of the retreat from world power. But only a part – and this leads me to my second theme. For the inability to hold on to empire was itself a reflection of more fundamental changes in the nature and distribution of power in the twentieth century.

The empire had been won at little cost. The British were far superior in weaponry to most of the non-whites they conquered. At the battle of Omdurman in 1898 Kitchener won the Sudan with the loss of only 368 men. His adversary, the Khalifa, lost 11,000 – massacred by 3500 shells and half a million bullets.[9] A half-century later, in 1946, a handful of Jewish insurgents, using seven milk churns packed with TNT, destroyed the King David Hotel in Jerusalem, nerve centre of British power in Palestine. Ninety-one died, and with them much of Britain's will to hold on to its troubled mandate.[10]

The spread of military technology also evened up the balance between Britain and its great-power rivals. Victoria's Pax Britannica was a creation of seapower. Being an island, Britain needed a large navy to defend its shores and to protect the foreign trade on which its prosperity depended. And its superior naval power enabled Britain to project its forces into every corner of the world, backed by a network of bases from Gibraltar to Singapore, from Simonstown to Hong Kong. Britain, in short, was the strongest and most mobile power of that technological era.

Britain's naval supremacy proved shortlived, however. In 1883 the Royal Navy had almost as many battleships as the rest of the world combined; in 1897 only two-thirds. First Germany, then America and Japan challenged its pre-eminence. By 1941 Britain was barely equal at sea to Japan alone.[11] Worse still, as the twentieth century progressed, the technology of warfare changed dramatically. Airpower replaced seapower as the decisive weapon, revolutionising mobility and rendering surface fleets largely impotent. In December 1941 the *Prince of Wales* and the *Repulse*, Britain's only capital ships in the Far East, were sunk in just two hours by Japanese torpedo bombers, leaving Britain's Asian empire virtually defenceless.[12]

Airpower not only shattered Britain's global supremacy, it also threatened the security of the British Isles themselves. In the age of seapower the English Channel had proved an insuperable barrier

2.3. The King David Hotel, Jerusalem, after the explosion

2.4. Bombers, Second
World War

against Philip II, Louis XIV and Napoleon. But the bomber changed
all that. In July 1934, Stanley Baldwin warned the House of
Commons that 'the old frontiers are gone. When you think of the
defence of England you no longer think of the chalk cliffs of Dover;
you think of the Rhine. That is where our frontier lies.'[13] In
September 1949, tests of atmospheric particles by British scientists
revealed an even grimmer danger: Britain's new adversary, Russia,
had an atomic bomb. The country was now vulnerable to airborne
destruction on a scale that made the Luftwaffe's raids on London or
Coventry seem trivial by comparison. Then from the late 1950s the
advent of ballistic missiles speeded up the potential delivery time of
these horrific weapons from hours to minutes. Britain could not hope
to stand alone against the nuclear and conventional might of the
Soviet Union. Its security, like that of Western Europe as a whole,
now depended on an Atlantic Alliance with the other nuclear giant,

the United States. What Shakespeare had called Britain's 'moat defensive' had become virtually irrelevant.

Of course, Britain did its best to keep up with these new military technologies. For instance, it became the world's third atomic power in 1952. But aircraft and nuclear weapons were far more expensive than machine guns and frigates, and here Britain's economic eclipse – my third theme – had an effect on its international power.

To some extent this was simply a matter of others catching up with Britain's initial lead as the first industrial nation. In 1860 Britain produced 20 per cent of the world's manufacturing output; in 1913 less than 14 per cent. Britain had been outstripped by America and Germany, the USA producing an astonishing 32 per cent of the world's total output by this date. Industrial strength was central to military power: after the First World War the British had to concede naval parity to the USA because they simply could not afford the costs of an all-out arms race with the world's strongest economy.

Yet we should not exaggerate Britain's economic predicament at this date. Although the British share of world manufactures rarely exceeded 10 per cent after 1913, Britain remained third in the league table of industrial output until the 1950s.[14] Relative industrial decline may therefore help to explain the limits of British power vis-à-vis America, Germany and Russia in the first half of this century. It tells us less about Britain's increasing impotence elsewhere. The problem, as we have seen, was that for any industrial state, however advanced, the twentieth-century world was much more difficult to mould because of the growth of rival powers and obstreperous dependents.[15]

As significant as raw industrial might was the country's financial position overseas. In 1900 Britain was the world's leading foreign investor, a position it retained despite growing American competition until after the Second World War. Iranian oil wells, Latin American railways, and Malayan rubber plantations were among its diverse assets. The ubiquity of Britain's trade and shipping also meant that many of its customers found it convenient to hold sterling in order to settle their international payments. Investment income and sterling balances helped generate the foreign exchange to pay for overseas commitments – the bases, troops, supplies and aid essential for Britain's global influence.

But Britain's overseas wealth gradually ebbed away, especially after 1945. The sterling crisis of early 1947 obliged the British to pull out abruptly from India, Palestine, Greece and Turkey. Another such crisis twenty years later forced the decision to withdraw almost entirely east of Suez. In part, Britain's foreign assets fell victim to the growing power of indigenous governments – Iranian oil was nationalised in 1951, likewise the Suez Canal in 1956. But even more important was the effect of two world wars. These utterly transformed Britain's overseas financial position.

In fact, the wars of 1914–18 and 1939–45 accelerated *all* the general trends that I have described – the rise of the superpowers, the loss of empire, the technological revolution in warfare, as well as the erosion of economic strength. We need now to look more closely at the dramatic impact of these great conflicts, particularly that of the Second World War.

Britain's position had been established by war and conquest – against the Dutch, the French and numerous native kingdoms. But by the end of Victoria's reign Great Britain had, literally, little to gain and everything to lose from further conflicts. Its exposed empire, its far-flung commerce, would all be imperilled by war. It was, of course, morally comforting to represent oneself as the great peace-loving power. The problem, as Winston Churchill observed, was that 'our claim to be left in unmolested enjoyment of vast and splendid possessions, mainly acquired by force, largely maintained by violence, often seems less reasonable to others than it does to us.'[16]

In the 1900s France, Russia and America were among those vying for pieces of Britain's empire. But the greatest threat of all was Germany, its main rival industrially and at sea, which demanded a position in the world commensurate with its new power and pretensions. This was a contest of ideologies as well as interests. Britain's liberal, anti-militarist values were pitted against Prussian autocracy in 1914–18 and in 1939–45 against its grotesque mutation – the genocidal imperialism of Adolf Hitler. Looking back, Churchill and others have depicted this whole period 1914–45 as another 'thirty years war', centred on Germany's double bid for hegemony.[17]

In round one, 1914–18, Britain emerged victorious. Germany was defeated, its fleet was destroyed, and in the 1920s the British Empire reached its largest extent as Britain expanded into the Middle East on the ruins of the old Ottoman empire. But victory had been won at a cost unimagined when Europe went gaily to war in August 1914. Instead of a rapid war of movement, over by Christmas, the conflict became a struggle between whole economies, fully mobilised for modern war. Against industrialised Germany – unlike Napoleonic France – Britain could not sustain itself and its allies unaided.

This became the dominant fact of the twentieth century for the British. If it came to total war, they could not defend their position as a great power without material and particularly financial help from the United States. When the reckoning was made in 1918, Britain had lost about 15 per cent of its national wealth, the USA had become a leading creditor nation, and Britain's American debt amounted to some $4.7 billion. In the late 1920s the British government was devoting almost 40 per cent of its annual budget to paying off its war debts, both at home and abroad.[18]

The costs of 1914–18 made British leaders all the more determined to avoid war in the 1930s when Hitler renewed Germany's bid for world power. Other considerations pointed in the same direction. After horrors like the Somme, pacifist sentiment waxed strong. The Treasury was sure that hasty rearmament would undermine foreign confidence in sterling and diminish British reserves, which were essential for the country's staying power in any war. Unlike the 1900s, there were no obvious allies – France was weak, America and Russia both seemed isolationist. And, again unlike the 1900s, Britain's other enemies, this time Italy and Japan, proved less easy to appease. Not until almost too late did Neville Chamberlain and his colleagues face up to the threat from Nazi Germany.

The Second World War upset the international balance of power far more profoundly than its predecessor. Hitler's astonishing victories in 1940–1 gave him complete control of continental Europe from the Bay of Biscay to the Black Sea. Britain was left alone, in grave danger of invasion. Then, in the winter of 1941–2, Japan's even more devastating successes brought it much of East and Southeast Asia. For a while even India and Australia were threatened. Unlike 1914–18, this was truly a world war. And the price for Britain as a world power was even higher.

Britain's prestige in its Asian empire never recovered from the humiliating defeats of 1941–2. Within two years of victory against Japan it had relinquished its position in India. Technologically, the war saw a desperate race to create an atomic bomb, as well as major developments in airpower such as saturation bombing and the jet engine. The economic demands of total war left Britain again dependent on American credits, Lend-Lease, as well as obliging it to dispose of 15 per cent of its foreign investments and to run up some £4 billion in debts within the Sterling Area. In all, the war reduced Britain's wealth by a quarter. Despite these sacrifices, however, and despite Britain's lonely resistance in 1940, victory over the Axis ultimately depended on the exertions of America and Russia. By mid-1945 these two new 'superpowers' were eyeing each other across the ruins of Hitler's Reich. Two years later, increasingly distrustful and unable to agree on the future of Germany, they began to divide not just Germany but most of Europe into their spheres of influence.

So the Second World War greatly accelerated the decline of Britain's world power. The same was true for the other major European states, all of whom suffered from the erosion of their empires and the rise of the superpowers. What is striking now is Britain's distinctive response to this general European predicament. Far more than any other

2.5. The surrender of
Singapore, 1942

2.6. The ruined city of
Stuttgart, 1945

2.7. The first meeting of the American and Russian armies, 1945

Western European state, even France, Britain was determined to maintain itself as a truly world power. This was a common policy of Labour and Conservative governments alike from the mid-1940s to the mid-1960s, of Ernest Bevin as much as Anthony Eden, of Harold Wilson as much as Winston Churchill. It was Wilson, as late as 1964, who insisted that 'we are a world power, and a world influence, or we are nothing'.[19] This determination to sustain a global role made Britain's adjustment to a changing world much harder than that of its neighbours.

British leaders were, of course, well aware in 1945 that they were no longer in the same league as America and Russia. They sometimes felt, as one diplomat put it, like 'Lepidus in the triumvirate with Mark Antony and Augustus'.[20] But Britain was unquestionably the leading European state, economically and militarily, and Whitehall believed it could hold on to world power by a twofold strategy. One way was to consolidate the informal empire. After 1945 London swam with the tide of decolonisation, but it also embarked on a programme of colonial economic development to increase Britain's overseas earnings through intensive production of Malayan tin and rubber, African ores, Middle Eastern oil, and other vital commodities. It also sought through negotiation to protect British assets and bases in key countries like Egypt and Iraq. The other foundation of global strategy was to cultivate what Churchill called a 'special relationship' with the USA.

2.8. Rebuilding Berlin, 1946

British leaders hoped to guide America, the new but immature world giant, by exploiting the special ties of language, culture and wartime friendships. Their object, as the Foreign Office put it condescendingly in 1944, was 'to make use of American power for purposes which we regard as good'.[21]

The continental states viewed the situation in the late 1940s very differently. Their experience of the Second World War was one of defeat, occupation and devastation. French and German leaders such as Jean Monnet and Konrad Adenauer saw the key to recovery not in the promotion of colonial trade but in a programme of industrial modernisation at home. Nothing of the sort occurred in Britain, where the experience of victory blinded many to the underlying changes in the world and Britain's place in it. Likewise, France, Germany, Italy and the Benelux countries came to see their salvation not in alliance with America, welcome though that was, but in cooperation among themselves. For them the lesson of 1940–5 was the need to bury the hatchet and work together. For Britain, by contrast, the war had confirmed its sense of alienation from the Continentals – foes or failed allies – and of kinship with what Churchill liked to call the 'English-speaking peoples' of America and the Commonwealth, who had helped win the ultimate victory. In 1950, for instance, the Labour Party insisted that 'in every respect except distance we in Britain are closer to our kinsmen in Australia and New Zealand on the far side of the world, than we are to Europe. We are closer in language and in origins, in social habits and institutions, in political outlook and in economic interest.'[22]

Britain, therefore, took little part in the movement for Western European integration, which culminated in the creation of the EEC in 1958. Plans for an inward-looking federal union seemed of little relevance to a world power. But during the 1950s the bankruptcy of its global strategy became apparent. Suez showed that even informal methods could not forestall the erosion of empire by nationalist regimes and also that America could not be relied on for automatic help in propping up British power. Equally disconcerting was the economic boom in Western Europe at a time when the Commonwealth and Sterling Area were stagnating. In 1961 Britain therefore applied to enter the EEC, only to be blocked for most of the decade by de Gaulle. By the time Britain did join in 1973 the Community had been shaped in the interests of the original Six, and reforms, for example on Britain's budget contribution, were particularly difficult at a time of world recession.

2.9. Britain enters the Common Market

Slowly since 1973 Britain has come to terms with its primarily European identity. That has not been easy. In parts of the Labour Party, suspicions of the EEC remain strong, while Mrs Thatcher has revived the idea of a special relationship with the USA. Much of the British public still conceives of 'Europe' as a collection of holiday resorts, wine lakes and butter mountains on the other side of the Channel. But British membership of the EEC is now no longer a matter of real political controversy, and in Whitehall planning has moved beyond economic integration to European political and military cooperation, especially with France and Germany.

By the 1970s, Britain was at last beginning to find a balance between its resources and its responsibilities. A global position acquired haphazardly when Britain was the world's leading economy and seapower had proved increasingly hard to defend against colonial nationalists and great-power rivals, particularly amidst rapid changes in military technology and the erosion of Britain's national wealth. Efforts to hang on to world power even after the pyrrhic victory of 1945 only further undermined the national economic interests that it was originally supposed to protect.[23] The 1967 decision to withdraw east of Suez and British entry into the EEC in 1973 represented major steps in adjusting policy to the limits of power. But responsibilities and resources are still not in equilibrium. In the 1980s the country continued to slide downhill economically, despite belated economic modernisation, and many defence analysts question whether, in its impoverished state, Britain can afford the costs of a nuclear role as well as extensive conventional commitments in Germany and the Atlantic.

Part of the problem is that even in this post-imperial age Britain's interests are not purely European. It still retains residual territorial obligations, such as Belize, Gibraltar, Hong Kong and, most intractable, the Falklands. Furthermore, Britain is still a major trading nation and, after the USA, the second largest foreign investor in the world. It is therefore vitally interested in the security of the sea lanes and the stability of areas such as Southeast Asia and the Middle East. Britain today is thus primarily but not exclusively a European power. Its interests are still inextricably bound up with the peace and prosperity of the wider world. But in the 1980s, unlike the 1870s, it can no longer afford to protect these interests unaided. Modern Britain is coping not only with the loss of its power and with its change of identity. It is also learning, painfully, to work with allies. The days of splendid isolation, like those of the Pax Britannica, are gone but their legacies are still with us.

Further Reading

Correlli Barnett, *The Collapse of British Power* (London, 1972); John Gallagher, *The Decline, Revival and Fall of the British Empire*, ed. Anil Seal (Cambridge, 1982); Michael Howard, *The Continental Commitment: The Dilemma of British Defence Policy in the Era of the Two World Wars* (Harmondsworth, 1974); Paul Kennedy, *The Realities behind Diplomacy: Background Influences on British External Policy, 1865–1980* (London, 1981); Bernard Porter, *Britain, Europe and the World, 1850–1986: Delusions of Grandeur* (London, 2nd edn, 1987); David Weigall, *Britain and the World, 1815–1986: A Dictionary of International Relations* (London, 1987).

The Decline of Britain?

Richard Overy

Britain's recent history has been dominated by the performance of the economy. Economic growth is the central issue of British politics, and it has become so for a good reason. In 1900 it was still possible to take British economic supremacy for granted. After a century and a half of almost uninterrupted growth, Britain was the centrepiece of the world economy, and the heart of a wealthy empire. Britain traded more than any other country, and possessed the world's largest merchant navy; the City of London invested more money overseas than the rest of the world put together. But since 1900 Britain has slowly declined from this position of pre-eminence, to become a small and comparatively less successful post-industrial economy. Political argument since at least the 1950s has been bound up with the so-called 'British disease', the slow erosion of Britain's economic strength and influence. Finding the cause and promoting the cure has become a major political priority.

Yet the simple economic fact is that the British economy has grown steadily, if unspectacularly, for most of the century. Average incomes are more than three times what they were in 1900. British industry by 1950 produced 100 per cent more than in 1913; by 1970 250 per cent more.[1] This paradox of apparent decline yet substantial growth can be readily explained. Other economies, richer in resources, larger in size, more efficient as producers, have grown faster and further than Britain. The British economy has not 'declined' since 1900, but has been eclipsed by economies that have, since then, fulfilled their economic potential. As the world economy got bigger it was inevitable that Britain's share in it would become relatively smaller.

A second explanation lies in the very uneven pattern of regional and industrial development within the overall growth of the economy. Entire areas and industries have declined at great social cost, fuelling a

3.1. Unemployed cotton workers, 1952

sense of crisis and loss. Indeed industry as a whole has declined relative to other sectors of the economy – the service sector, government employment, even agriculture. Britain is now experiencing de-industrialisation, a re-routing of economic strength from the older industrial regions of the North, Scotland, Wales and the Midlands, to the prosperous new service and 'hi-tech' communities of the South. The fruits of economic growth over the century have been spread very unevenly across the country, and between different social groups. A cycle of decline and renewal has been the major feature of Britain's recent economic experience.

In 1900 Lancashire was still the heart of Britain's industrial economy. Bolton was a typical product of this early industrialisation. Close to the Lancashire coalfield, it specialised in cotton-spinning and weaving, exporting its products all over the world. It was the site of the famous Soho works which produced some of the country's early steam engines. But in the 1920s Bolton, like the other cotton towns, was under threat. Competition abroad, excess capacity at home, and a lack of modern equipment and large mills led to the gradual erosion of the cotton trade. Bolton's firms were forced by the banks to whom they owed large sums of money to amalgamate to survive, but the decline was remorseless. During the war many mills were forced to close altogether, and by 1950 45 per cent of the cotton workers in Bolton were unemployed. Where cotton workers had made up almost two-thirds of the workforce in 1929, the figure was only a third in 1950.[2]

decline of old staples

But while the towns of the first industrial revolution saw their traditional industries decline, towns further to the south, away from the sea and the coal, saw increasing prosperity and the growth of a wave of new industries. Coventry, nicknamed the 'British Detroit', was very much the product of the so-called 'second industrial revolution', the industrial boom based on consumer durables, chemicals and electricity. At the end of the nineteenth century Coventry was the home of a whole range of small metal and craft trades. It was a centre for silk and watch manufacture. But these artisan traditions made it the ideal site for the new consumer industries, bicycles and then motor-cars, and for specialised machinery and machine-tools. Migrant labour from the surrounding villages and small towns flowed into the car factories of Humber, Singer, Rover, Standard and Daimler. The First World War completed the transformation, as the car firms were converted to produce aircraft and munitions. In the inter-war years Coventry was a major centre of car production, aviation, the electrical industry and heavy machinery; it was also Britain's fastest growing city, almost doubling its population between the wars. It was the twentieth-century boom town equivalent of the cotton towns of the eighteenth century. After 1945 it consolidated its leading position as a manufacturer of vehicles, machine-tools and aeronautical equipment.

But in the 1960s the boom turned sour. The collapse of British military aviation brought the loss of 11,000 jobs in five years. The car industry began to slow down, profits slumped, and in the 1970s it went into sharp decline. From 1975 to 1982 Coventry lost two-thirds of its workforce in motor vehicles. Alfred Herbert Ltd, the most famous Coventry machine-builder, was given state aid in the 1970s, but could not be saved and was wound up in 1983, with a workforce of only 400 instead of the 12,000 of the early 1970s. Fifty years after Coventry became the 'British Detroit' much of it is now an industrial wasteland.[3]

Of course the collapse of cotton in Bolton, or cars in Coventry, has not meant the collapse of the city's entire economy. They have both diversified their production, and industry is much less important than it once was. But they are no longer the typical cities of their time. The centres of the age of de-industrialisation are to be found in the south of the country; places like Milton Keynes, Bracknell or Cambridge, where the employment structure is highly diversified, where industry is concentrated in 'hi-tech' sectors, in electronics or specialised industrial services, but where much of the local employment comes in the service sectors, tourism, retailing and government or local administration. Bracknell has the lowest unemployment in the country. Cambridge has been transformed in twenty years from a market town built

3.2. Engineering
workshop, Coventry,
before First World War

around its university, to one of the centres of science-based industry, with an enormous tourist sector, high levels of educational employment and new science parks. Industry in the old sense has played only a small part in this change. The industries that Cambridge did once boast, such as Pye, the major radio and television manufacturer of the 1950s and 1960s, have almost disappeared. But the city is more prosperous than it ever was, a symbol of the transition from the industrial towns of the North and Midlands to the post-industrial towns of the South. Each stage in this progression has brought a large share of social hardship, high unemployment in particular, but at the point of every major decline the British economy has adjusted to the new market conditions and continued to grow.

The classic example of this phenomenon, of the intermingling of growth and decline, of poverty and plenty, was the slump of the 1930s. This contrast was captured well by the novelist George Orwell with his two books *The Road to Wigan Pier* and *Coming up for Air* — the one with its bleak description of a region hit by unemployment and industrial decline, the other with its wryly optimistic view of the new light-industrial towns of the South, with their suburban villas and new white-collar workforce.

The first of these images is familiar enough: the Jarrow Crusade for jobs, the idle dockyards and looms, the depressed regions which the government defined as 'Special Areas'. The reasons for this collapse could be found before the First World War. Britain was the first nation to industrialise, and remained committed as a result to old industrial locations, old work methods and equipment, for much longer than her leading competitors. Only the strength of Britain's position as financier and shipper masked how rapidly the competitive lead Britain once enjoyed was challenged by Germany, America and Japan. During the war Britain found her traditional markets eroded by industrialisation elsewhere. In the 1920s Britain was overcommitted to industries which could no longer compete against cheaper rivals. The shipping industry was ruined by the glut of wartime shipbuilding and the fall in world trade after 1920. Iron and steel, chemicals, textiles, engineering were hampered by old-fashioned work-practices and restrictions, by factories and furnaces that were too small, and by the fierce independence and poor market awareness of many British businessmen, the men Keynes found 'insensitive, stale, unadaptable'. The poor industrial relations of the 1920s, symbolised by the General Strike in 1926, were a product of growing tension between a workforce anxious to maintain its gains and protect its skills, and employers who saw low wages as the only way to combat shrinking markets and falling profits. The depression in 1929 completed the process of decline. Towns in Lancashire, South Wales, Tyneside,

3.3. Suburban housing, 1930

3.4. Jarrow marchers

lowland Scotland, the heartlands of the classical industrial revolution, experienced levels of unemployment up to 70 per cent of the workforce. Though there was modest recovery in the 1930s, and even something of a post-war boom after 1945, the days of the old regions were numbered and they have remained the least buoyant parts of the United Kingdom economy ever since.[4]

But the impact of the recession in these areas was in sharp contrast to the overall performance of the economy. The British economy grew faster in the 1930s than any other major economy save Hitler's Germany. The engine of growth was the rapid increase in real income, a result of falling food prices, cheap imports and rising wages; a result, too, of major improvements in productivity as firms gradually adjusted to the more hostile market conditions by adopting new production methods. Average earnings increased in real terms by 30 per cent between 1920 and 1938.[5] The extra money was spent not on the old industries, which had been export-orientated, but on new consumer industries at home, or on new services. One of these services was retailing which was revolutionised with the coming of chain shops and department stores: Boots, Home & Colonial, Marks & Spencer or Woolworths. In 1900 there were 290,000 shops, in 1939 half a million. Retailing employed more than coal-mining or cotton by 1939.[6]

There was also a marked regional shift. The new expanding industries, no longer dependent on water power, or the ports, or coal and iron, were located close to the sources of cheap labour, or the large urban markets, or the skilled workforce of the small manufacturing centres in the Midlands. Many of the new industries were distinguished not only by their modern products (cars, radios), but by the way they were made, in larger factories by more modern production methods. Contemporaries called this 'Fordism', mass-production along the lines pioneered by the American car producer, Henry Ford.

One of the best examples of this new direction was the growth of the Morris car empire around Oxford and the south Midlands between the wars. Morris was Britain's Henry Ford, pioneering motoring for the masses, selling his cars energetically through promotional advertising and hire-purchase schemes. In 1919 Morris produced 387 cars. By 1923 he was producing 20,000, by 1935 almost 100,000. He became Britain's largest producer, and Britain's richest manufacturer. Morris Motors was also a different kind of company, buying up its major suppliers and taking over weaker rivals. What began as a small owner-manager business became within twenty years a modern industrial corporation, with a wide network of businesses in Britain and overseas.[7] The car industry as a whole

3.5. The Morris garage in Oxford, 1902

3.6. The Morris headquarters, 1919

increased output tenfold in a generation. Like the electronics industry, aircraft and chemicals it contributed to the rapid modernisation of Britain's productive economy at just the point that the old staples were in decline. The two curves crossed in the 1930s. During the Second World War demand for the modern industries enormously expanded and it was these new sectors, and new services that maintained economic growth after 1945.

Very much the same sort of thing has happened again in the 1970s. The long post-war boom faltered in the more competitive climate of the 1960s and then, during the following ten years, the major industries that had led the new wave of growth faced serious crisis themselves. Britain entered a phase of de-industrialisation: the run-down and closure of factories in a very short period of time, which only twenty years before had been at the core of Britain's post-war boom. The car industry faced a flood of foreign imports after 1973. British Leyland, itself an amalgamation of some of Britain's largest vehicle producers, was forced to go to the government to save it from collapse in 1974. The aeronautical industry faced the same problems, with large-scale redundancies in the 1960s in the face of competition from American producers and the cuts in British defence expenditure. Again it was nationalisation that kept the industry going at all during the 1970s. The production of televisions and radios has gone overseas, although in the 1950s Britain was one of the major producers and exporters. Mullards, Britain's largest maker of radio components, produced 3.5 million valves in 1947, 40 million in 1966, but was closed down in 1981.[8]

The fate of a firm like Mullards shows how complete has been the decline in key sectors of the 'second industrial revolution'. The second wave of collapse has produced very much the same social effects as in the 1930s – high unemployment, regional decline, large pockets of social deprivation. But the causes were not necessarily the same. At the end of the Second World War, at the start of the great boom, the outlook was far from gloomy. This time three of Britain's major trade rivals, Germany, Italy and Japan, were in ruins. The war had improved British technology and modernised the factories. The government's extensive control over the whole economy in wartime was not entirely dismantled and the 'Keynesian Revolution', the belief that government action could keep up levels of demand at home and prevent further slumps like 1929, became the new orthodoxy. Demand at home and abroad was buoyant as Britain filled the gaps in world trade. But this very initial success bred a kind of complacency in British producers, a search for the quick short-term profit. Not enough attention was given to the longer-term strategy necessary to combat the continued rise of other competing industrial economies as they

3.7. The Morris headquarters in the 1920s

3.8. An advertisement for Morris cars, 1929

recovered from the effects of war. Britain failed to invest enough in new technologies or new products, so that her productivity declined sharply against her rivals. By 1973 Britain's largest car producer, British Leyland, could produce only 5 cars a year for every worker; Renault and Opel produced over 14, Peugeot 12 and Volkswagen 10. There were growing problems too of overmanning and outdated labour practices. During the boom period British managers were happy to accept these and to pay high wages to buy industrial peace. But by the 1960s these policies also damaged Britain's competitiveness. The result was a fall in the export of leading manufactured products and an increase in cheaper or better quality imports, creating regular balance-of-payments problems and a weak pound.[9] The 1973 oil crisis and the onset of high levels of inflation only completed a process of industrial crisis and low growth already evident in the 1960s.

Yet once again it would be misleading to see this often catastrophic collapse of key industries as a reversal of economic growth. As in the 1930s two curves crossed in the 1970s. The declining industries streamlined themselves where possible, introduced new products or new work methods in order to salvage something from the crisis. Other, newer, industries expanded rapidly: modern electronics at 17 per cent a year; or the chemical industry, constantly adapting itself to new demands and new products, which grew four times faster during the 1970s than the rest of industry. In the 1980s industrial survival has depended on extensive rationalisation and effective marketing. Trade has been helped by selling North Sea oil. Weaker sectors have continued to rely on high levels of government subsidy.

More significant, the crisis of the 1970s showed the extent to which Britain is much less dependent on industry for economic growth than in the 1930s. More people now work in white-collar occupations than in manufacturing. Retailing employs 3 million people. Other services have greatly expanded. Leisure has become a major sector in its own right, embracing sectors as diverse as tourism and pop music. Administration is a major source of employment. Even farming, left to decline in the heyday of Victorian industry, has become an important modernised sector, though dependent since the 1930s on government subsidies, and since 1973, on Common Market payments.[10] Industry is now only one part of an increasingly diversified economy with new sources of growth. The real importance of industry in the 1980s lies in its ability to earn money overseas to pay for imports. The 'service economy', which many economists now believe Britain is becoming, cannot survive without industry. The recent weaknesses of British industry have thus created an economy precariously balanced between the new boom and the prospect of serious crisis.

It would, of course, be wrong to suggest that Britain has simply been at the mercy of blind market forces, to which she has been compelled belatedly, and at great social cost, to adjust. There are factors that have operated over the whole century to encourage economic growth and to mitigate the impact of the market. The first of these, and certainly the most important, has been the changing role of government. In its simplest terms the government spent twice as much in the inter-war years as it did before 1914, and twice as much in the 1950s as it did in the 1930s.[11] Government is also an enormous employer of labour. In 1980 almost one in three of the employed workforce worked for central and local government, or in state industries. This has helped to maintain high levels of demand in the economy, and to promote investment. But this is not all that the state has done. Since the First World War governments have gradually become more involved in industry and trade, through tariffs, programmes of state-sponsored rationalisation, or state ownership of mines or railways. The government provided extensive subsidies for industry and farms, and has improved education and training; it has also taken a leading role, certainly since 1945, in regulating periodically some of the major elements of economic activity – prices and wages in the 1960s and 1970s, interest rates, patterns of industrial location, even the export of goods and capital. This has not always had entirely fortunate results, and governments have fought shy of long-term planning for the economy, but without the involvement of government the economy would almost certainly have experienced much more serious problems in the inter-war years or in the 1970s.[12]

A second factor running right through the whole period has been the growing importance of science and technology. There has been a marked shift over the century away from the production of large quantities of cheap goods to the production of high-quality and more expensive products. For the industrial economies of Europe this was an essential shift, for they could not compete with low-wage, low-cost economies in the production of mass consumer goods. Instead they have applied modern science directly to industry, and used more sophisticated technology. Britain's record in this respect has been a mixed one. Britain has proved to be a great source of invention (radar, the hovercraft, jet engines, television etc.), but has not always been quick to innovate, to use the new discoveries for full commercial advantage. But if progress has been uneven it has been more or less continuous. Qualitative improvements have allowed even the declining industries in the 1930s or the 1970s to adapt sufficiently to avoid complete collapse. Cottonmakers produced rayon and cellophane after the war; radio producers now work on components for satellites.

Finally British capitalism itself has undergone something of a revolution over the century. The small family firm which dominated British industry in the early 1900s has given way to the giant corporation, linked with the world of multinational enterprise, with a new style of management and a highly-trained workforce.[13] The modernisation of British industry and finance has proceeded inexorably if slowly over the period. Only recently has the historic divide between British finance, centred on the City, and British industry been bridged. Industrial capitalism in America, or Germany or Japan, has benefited from the close links between banks and firms which encouraged high levels of direct industrial investment and better productivity. Historically British business has been hampered not only by this long-term distinction between industrial and finance capital, but by the conservatism of much of the traditional business community.

These problems bring us back to the question we started with: why do people feel that Britain's economy since 1900 has been a story of decline?[14] It is because other economies have grown faster than Britain's, and have survived the harsher climate of competition over the last twenty years more successfully. Japan and West Germany, those very economies laid waste in 1945, have long overtaken Britain in any measurement of economic performance. They have lower levels of unemployment and inflation, higher wages and better sales records. Britain's economic history over this period tells us at least something about why this has happened. Britain's market responses, particularly in the 1920s and again in the 1950s, were sluggish and complacent. A great many captains of industry have gone down with their ships rather than make a change of course in time. Britain's industries came from a background of small-scale, fiercely independent businesses, wedded to established practices and markets. Traditions of practical craftsmanship, of cautious investment, of managerial paternalism dominated British industry, and lingered on into an age when these qualities were a positive handicap to further expansion. The commercial traditions were of short-term risk and slow profit growth. Such a cast of mind adjusted only with great difficulty to the world of big industry, long-term planning and vigorous selling.

This problem of selling has been a persistent theme in criticism of British industry since the crisis over 'Made in Germany' in the 1890s. It has been the result of the curious social and functional divisions in the British economy. Within industrial firms the practical man, the engineer and inventor, traditionally enjoyed higher status than the salesman. The commercial side of British industry attracted less qualified managers; and commercial education has, historically, been limited and undervalued, as has vocational training in general. Commerce was respectable only when divorced from industry altogether, in the City of London, where it involved trade in major commodities such as cotton or tea, or in stocks and shares. These commercial weaknesses in industry were most marked overseas. Where before 1914 German and American firms sent large and well-prepared sales teams abroad, armed with good economic intelligence, Britain's trade was often conducted by poorly-qualified local agents, or by correspondence alone. This pattern persisted long afterwards. A lack of professionalism, combined with the very limited number of salesmen detailed to work overseas, and the absence of good economic intelligence on foreign markets, was reflected in the rapid undermining of British trade in the 1920s and again in the 1950s and 1960s. Even William Morris, so successful in the context of the British market, experienced his first major failure with the 'Empire Car' launched in the late 1920s, which failed entirely to meet the technical requirements of the empire areas it was destined for. After 1945 the sales boom of British vehicles abroad came to an end because of their poor adaptation to local market conditions, and the persistent failure to provide adequate after-sales service.

But a more fundamental explanation of this commercial failure lies in the nature of the historical circumstances facing British producers. They simply lacked the market pressures to sell more vigorously for much of the century. Before 1914 the long years of British financial and naval supremacy created a sheltered environment for many British traders. Britain could provide credit, and could transport and insure goods, on such a scale that British industry enjoyed a head-start over many rivals. In the 1920s and 1930s many of the new industries were protected by tariffs or international cartel agreements, which encouraged the rapid expansion of the home market, but removed some of the pressure to compete more effectively with foreign goods. In the long post-war boom after 1945, Britain benefited from the collapse of most potential rivals, and operated in a seller's market; but Britain's major competitors across this period could only succeed, not just by producing cheaper or better products, but by selling them more energetically abroad. The general protection given to British producers by market conditions helped to sustain the low status of the salesman and the imbalance between production and commerce that grew up with Victorian industrial society.

There were problems, too, with labour. Because of Britain's early start, workers were already well organised by the late nineteenth century and attached to patterns of demarcation and skill which matched the traditions of the small workshop, or the shipyards or the mines. The decline of these skills, with the changing nature of employment and technology, put labour onto the defensive for much of the period. This in turn exacerbated the relatively poor relations between employers and employees, which were embodied in the early emergence of very clear class divisions in British society. These habits of confrontation and defence of interests were carried over into the world of large-scale business and modern capitalism after 1945, and acted as a significant brake on the transformation of the economy during the long post-war boom. Only in the last ten years has Britain begun, slowly, to shed the residue of her industrial heritage and the penalties of being the first industrial society.

Finally, there is no doubt that British society has had a very ambiguous relationship with its economy. Where business success in Japan or West Germany or America is at the centre of social ambition and social status, it has always had to compete in Britain in a complex structure of status and snobbery, in which 'trade' as distinct from banking, or landownership, or the professions, has never quite been accepted. The vulgar pursuit of possessions, though it is indeed the engine of modern economic growth, has never been wholeheartedly accepted in British culture. For a great deal of the century Britain has been the gentleman and the others merely players. The Victorian values of hardy individualism, of thrift and gentility, of the dislike of display and excess, have cast a long shadow into the modern age.

Further Reading

D. Aldcroft, *The British Economy between the Wars* (Oxford, 1983); B.W. Alford, *Depression and Recovery? British Economic Growth 1918–1939* (London, 1972); G. Allen, *British Industries and their Organization* (London, 1959); R. Floud and D. McCloskey, *The Economic History of Britain since 1700*, vol. 2 (Cambridge, 1981); M.W. Kirby, *The Decline of British Economic Power since 1870* (London, 1981); P. Pagnamenta and R.J. Overy, *All Our Working Lives* (London, 1984); M.H. Peston, *The British Economy* (Oxford, 1982); S. Pollard, *The Development of the British Economy 1914–1967* (London, 1969); L.J. Williams, *Britain and the World Economy 1919–1970* (London, 1971); A.J. Youngson, *Britain's Economic Growth 1920–1966* (London, 1967).

CHAPTER
FOUR

The New Jerusalem

John Stevenson

On 4 January 1941, with the Battle of Britain only just won and the blitz still raging, the popular magazine, *Picture Post*, published a special edition under the title 'A Plan for Britain'. Between the advertisements for Brylcreem and Bile Beans lay a prospectus for a new Britain, a series of articles putting forward radical new proposals for a completely fresh approach to employment, social welfare, housing, town planning, the countryside, health and education. Most striking of all, perhaps, were the ambitious sketches for the 'new town' of the future, with its blocks of flats, its American-style highways and flyovers, and the strict separation of the new city into different zones for housing, leisure and industry. 'The new Britain must be Planned' was the headline under which the leading young architect Maxwell Fry contrasted the haphazard squalor of the typical pre-war British city with its slums, its unplanned development, and its gross pollution of air and water with the bright new hope for the future expressed in the plans and drawings of the architects and town planners.[1]

These proposals, with their aspirations for a better tomorrow, contained in a popular picture magazine, caught a particular mood in wartime Britain. They illustrated dramatically the desire for something better after the war was won. The 'Plan for Britain' represented a virtual glossary of progressive ideas current in pre-war Britain and its various contributors were a fair cross-section of the high-minded and socially-concerned individuals who had campaigned on behalf of a better future even before the war broke out. The war was only the occasion for the expression of advanced ideas about the shape of British society in the years to come and which found its opportunity in the shared perils and challenges of the early years of the Second World War. But as well as expressing a mood, these plans also revealed a

4.1. Industrial pollution, 1930s

style. In their stress upon planning and rational solutions to social problems they represented a set of attitudes which have, for better or worse, shaped the Britain in which we live.

Few ideas have had more influence upon Britain in the twentieth century than the belief that social problems were susceptible to scientific analysis and rational solutions based upon their investigation. And perhaps nowhere have these ideas witnessed a more precipitate rise and fall than in the attempts to build, quite literally, a new Britain. From the end of the nineteenth century, social reformers believed that poor housing, insanitary conditions and overcrowded towns and cities created poverty, crime and immorality. Only the creation of a better environment – rebuilt and planned – could cure the ills of industrial society. A century later, in the 1980s, that reshaped physical environment was blamed for precisely those problems it was designed to abolish forever. How was this faith in a planned 'New Jerusalem' created and where did it go wrong?

Belief in the therapeutic value of the environment was one of the most important contributions of the late nineteenth century to twentieth-century social thinking. But it developed only slowly. For much of the Victorian period the dominant sentiment was that poverty, crime and immorality were the products of moral deficiency and innate weaknesses of character. One of the most influential popularisers of what we now think of as Victorian values, Samuel Smiles, whose best seller *Self-Help* was published in 1859, preached the gospel of sturdy independence and individual effort. For Smiles, national progress was the sum of individual industry, energy and perseverance just as national decay was the sum of individual idleness, selfishness and vice. Poverty and squalor were to a large degree self-inflicted, saving only the obviously infirm and helpless; self-help through individual effort and self-improvement, thrift, and prudent restraint of the animal appetites was a ladder that all could climb. Smiles and those who thought like him explicitly denied that social improvement was a matter for better laws and institutions. Action taken on behalf of individuals was enfeebling and demoralising, rendering the recipients passive and dependent, and removing the spur to individual effort — what law, however stringent, could make the idle industrious, the thriftless provident, or the drunken sober?[2]

Such views, however, were to come under serious challenge by the end of the nineteenth century and with it came a much greater stress upon the role of the environment in shaping the character and behaviour of individuals. The late nineteenth century was remarkable for the 'rediscovery of poverty', as a wave of social investigators set out to explore the dimensions and causes of the poverty and squalor which remained an all too obvious feature of late Victorian Britain. The first serious statistical surveys of social problems by men such as Charles Booth and Seebohm Rowntree brought to bear pioneering techniques of social investigation about the scale and causes of social problems such as poverty and inadequate housing. Charles Booth produced a magisterial survey of the *Life and Labour of the People of London* in which he was able to document street by street what he called the 'Arithmetic of Woe', revealing that almost a third of the population was living in poverty. It was another Booth, General William Booth of the Salvation Army, who provided the passion to go with the statistics. In his *In Darkest England and the Way Out* he urged Victorians to turn aside from the problems of the dark continent of Africa to investigate more closely than they had hitherto the misery and destitution which lay on their own doorsteps. It was General Booth who delivered a crushing rebuke to those who called on the poor to pull themselves up by their own bootstraps through the practice of the virtues of self-help and thrift: 'What is the use', he wrote, 'of the Gospel of Thrift to a man who had nothing to eat yesterday, and has not threepence today to pay for his lodging tonight? To live on nothing a day is difficult enough, but to save on it would best the cleverest political economist that ever lived.'[3]

But in terms of attitudes towards social policy, the real cutting edge had to be provided by the more sober and systematic studies of poverty and squalor. A whole generation of people going into social investigation in the late Victorian and Edwardian era shared a spirit of rational optimism based upon the proved advances of science, a belief in progress, and a socialist or a Christian commitment to the betterment of their fellow men. The young Beatrice Webb, one of the founders of the Fabian movement, cut her teeth as a social investigator helping Charles Booth in his surveys of the East End; Eleanor Rathbone, a leading advocate of family allowances in the twentieth century, had studied the appalling squalor of the Liverpool slums and never forgotten it. Something of the tone of these pioneers was expressed by Lord Woolton, later well known as Minister of Food in the Second World War, who recalled that when he went down from university in the years before the First World War to undertake social survey work in the slums, he did so in order to find the answer to the question 'Why are so many people poor?' For him the investigation of poverty took on the same character as that of the medical scientist enquiring into the causes of a disease, to which an effective cure could then be found.[4]

These people were amongst the founding fathers – and mothers – of a British school of social science based upon empirical observation of social problems. They provided the tools by which social problems could be measured and, implicitly, solved. Booth and Rowntree devised 'povery lines' and 'standards of human needs' to investigate the exact dimensions of social problems. Rowntree's study of York in 1899 was formulated on the basis of a standard of human needs which meant the income required to provide food, rent and clothing for each member of a family. He was able to refine his standard of human needs in subsequent investigations to take account of improved knowledge about nutrition, still a science in its infancy prior to 1914.[5] The importance of these new techniques of social investigation was manifold. Applying the same techniques to housing and health provided measures of overcrowding and density of settlement in the slum districts. They provided the statistics on infant mortality and deaths from tuberculosis, which it was only natural that people should begin to match up with the map of poverty and overcrowding.

As a result, social problems could be targeted more precisely than ever before. Claims of the personal irresponsibility of the poor could now be tested against hard evidence, evidence which increasingly suggested that the poor themselves could do very little to solve those social problems that beset them. Once social conditions had been surveyed and diagnosed, wise remedial legislation could be produced.

By 1914, a burst of social legislation had met some of the social problems mapped out by the social investigators with the provision of old age pensions for the elderly, and social insurance to guard against some of the obvious calamities which could plunge families into destitution: sickness, accidents and unemployment. But there remained the very much larger question of how the quality of life could be improved and basic standards of human decency maintained in the grim, insanitary legacy of the industrial revolution.

One of the recurrent themes of nineteenth-century social investigation which flowed into the social thought of the twentieth was that a more salubrious environment had a crucial part to play in improving not only the quality of life but also the very character of individuals. Victorian interest in public health was not merely a matter of clean water and better drains for their own sake, but because they saw them as important for the improvement of the tenor of people's lives. Piped water and flush toilets were important weapons in leading to clean living and better morals. Similarly, overcrowded dwellings which obliged parents to share the same bedroom with their children or forced grown-up brothers and sisters to share the same room and even the same bed were a frequent cause of concern. Incest and child-abuse, fashionable causes today, were never far from the minds of social investigators who penetrated the garrets, cellars and slum tenements of Britain's towns and cities. Medical experts, too, were concerned by insanitary dwellings, squalid outside toilets shared by several families, damp, poorly ventilated houses, achingly cold in winter and humid and foetid in summer. Tuberculosis, one of the great health scourges of the early twentieth century, was already recognised as a disease which flourished in poorly ventilated tenements and courts. Infectious disease of every kind spread like wildfire in the overcrowded slums, producing epidemics of diphtheria, measles, influenza, scarlet fever and whooping cough which still carried off thousands of children every year.

Given half a chance, the poor and the slumdwellers could tell their own story, of the daily battles with dirt, damp and vermin – the rats, cockroaches and bugs that were the accompaniment of poor housing in most of the major cities and towns. Few who ever encountered it could forget the smell of damp, decaying property in which literally millions of people had to live their lives.[6] Moreover the slum districts were usually sited cheek by jowl with the factories, ports and mines in which people earned their living. Industry, transport and domestic dwellings poured forth a fearful blanket of smoke and other pollutants. One needs only to look at old photographs of the industrial districts of Britain to appreciate to what extent even up to and beyond the Second World War they suffered from gross pollution of the atmosphere, bringing with it an almost inevitable catalogue of respiratory disease, such as bronchitis, and the terrible smogs which could kill thousands of people whose health was already hanging by a thread because of the filthy environment they had inhabited all their lives. It was hardly surprising that turn-of-the-century visionaries looked to a clean future, with clear, fresh air, sparkling rivers teeming with fish – a healthy environment freed from the worst that the industrial revolution had wrought.

Hence many sought ways not only of easing the poverty which bedevilled the lives of so many of the lower classes in early twentieth-century Britain, but also of creating a totally remodelled environment in which clean, healthy lives could be lived to the full. Few ideas, perhaps none, have so captured the imagination of well-meaning people as that of recreating a truly green and pleasant land on the ruin and desolation of the past. Utopian visions of this type were not uncommon in the nineteenth century, when the Chartists and other groups of pioneers had hoped to set up self-sufficient settlements in the countryside, abandoning the squalor and filth of industrialisation altogether. There was a revival of interest in these ideas in the early twentieth century. The first genuine experiment with a new type of planned environment came with the 'garden city' movement associated with the name of Ebenezer Howard. Howard aimed to combine the best of town and country in a medium-sized city situated in the

4.2. An artist's impression of Letchworth Garden City

4.3. One of
Letchworth's tree-lined
streets

4.4. Housing for
munitions workers at
Well Hall, Eltham

countryside, surrounded by a 'green belt', which it was hoped would attract people from the overcrowded towns into a healthier, cleaner environment. Letchworth, the first Garden City, was started on a self-financing basis in 1903 and by 1914 had a population of almost 9000.[7] Howard's ideas were enormously influential and led to a number of experiments with the building of garden suburbs, which if not quite in line with Howard's original plans, tried to recreate on a few private estates a pleasant, semi-rural environment with good-quality housing.

The difficulty was that these experiments were self-financing and of necessity limited. They came nowhere near a solution for the millions of slumdwellers in the great cities. The First World War, however, marked a major advance. As in many other spheres, it led to government intervention, in providing housing for munitions workers in places such as Gretna in Scotland and Well Hall near Eltham in London. The estates borrowed the best planning principles and house-layouts available. Great stress was placed upon providing space, light and ventilation, an adequate number of bedrooms for each family, and separate kitchens and bathrooms. These first steps by the government into providing good-quality housing were important because hitherto housebuilding had been largely left to local authorities and philanthrophic initiative and on the whole little had been achieved. The war, however, led to more than a few housing estates for munitions workers. In the battle for domestic morale in the dark days of 1917 and 1918, the Lloyd George government offered its war-weary troops and civilians a world worth all the pain and sacrifice, by inaugurating its famous scheme of 'homes fit for heroes'.[8] In the Addison Housing Acts passed just after the Great War, the government offered generous subsidies to both private and council house building. Good-quality housing for the masses was the aim, following the pattern of the 'garden city' idealists and the wartime estates.

Unfortunately, although the Addison Acts established government responsibility for housing as a major priority, the scheme had to be halted because of financial cut-backs with the onset of the depression. None the less, a series of further Housing Acts in the inter-war years, on a rather less generous scale than provided for in 1918, began to make some impact on the worst of the slums. During the great housing boom of the 1930s, when private builders were providing cheap 'semis' by the million to house the middle classes in the growing suburbs, local authorities were encouraged to borrow money and engage in slum clearance and rehousing.

By any standard the results were impressive. Between 1931 and 1939 local authorities cleared a quarter of a million slum properties

4.5. Old Wythenshawe, Manchester

and built over 700,000 houses. Much of this new housing was built as a somewhat diluted version of the 'garden suburb' as extensive estates on the fringes of the main towns and cities, at Kirkby, near Liverpool, Solihull and Longbridge outside Birmingham, and in a series of estates around London. The best of them, like the satellite town of Wythenshawe, built to the south of Manchester, really did offer a fair attempt at capturing something of the pleasant, semi-rural atmosphere of the 'garden city' with tree-lined avenues, spacious verges and extensive open spaces. But others were built on the cheap, with more of an eye to quantity than quality. Many estates provided little in the way of amenities – lacking communal facilities such as pubs, shops and meeting places. It was reported that some of the Liverpool council estates had been built deliberately without provision for any licensed premises in the hope of discouraging the 'demon drink'. The chief results were only a healthy trade in bottled beer and lengthy treks to the only available public houses outside the sober reach of the council's jurisdiction.[9] Women, in particular, were affected by the disruption of family ties, stranding young families miles from their relatives and much-needed emotional support. Few, if any, architects and planners had much idea of the network of mutual support and kinship which was such an important feature of economic and social survival in the slums, neither did they understand the informal

4.6. Workers' flats in
Vienna, built 1919

4.7. Quarry Hill Flats,
Leeds

grapevines of information about jobs, borrowing of tools and money, and exchange of help which were very difficult to re-establish from scratch in the new housing estates.

In some places, local authorities were beginning their first experiments with flats, often modelled upon similar developments in continental cities. Workers' housing in cities such as Vienna looked attractive to young planners and architects who were beginning to be influenced by the modern movement in architecture. They seemed to offer cheap, mass housing, in which adequate services could be sited to meet the needs of a whole community. At Leeds, the municipality pioneered the construction of flats in the Quarry Hill scheme near the centre of the city, where 2000 slum houses were demolished and replaced by a giant block of 938 flats at a cost of £1.5m. Less ambitious schemes of three and four-storey maisonettes also made their appearance in some of the inner city areas, such as Hulme in Manchester, where land was scarce and rehousing necessitated building upwards. At this stage, however, the debate between houses and flats, between low-rise and high-rise, tended to side with the traditional forms of construction. Those with experience of the sheer awfulness of the slums were ready to accept that the new estates were not always perfect, but saw them for what they undoubtedly were — a quantum leap in terms of physical amenities from what had existed before. Touring the council estates of York in the 1930s, Seebohm Rowntree could barely contain his delight in the way the rehoused slumdwellers had turned the rough land surrounding their new houses into beautiful gardens. Sir Ernest Simon, lord mayor of Manchester, and a prolific writer on housing questions, as well as the founder of the Wythenshawe estate, was in no doubt that people could 'make good' in their new environment. He solemnly rebutted some of the stories about the misuse of sanitary facilities by the new council tenants — not a single instance could he find of a bath being used for any purpose other than that for which it was intended![10]

The inter-war years undoubtedly saw some major advances. But on the eve of the Second World War, a new generation of architects and planners were beginning to champion much more extensive remodelling of the physical environment. The rise of the motor car required new roads and plans for traffic management. As well as the old concerns with rehousing the slumdwellers, this helped to give a spur to ambitious ideas for wholesale town planning. The experience of unregulated building in the private housing sector with its ribbon development and 'bungaloid' growth and the seemingly unchecked construction in the south-east of England in the boom years of the late 1930s, seemed to demand vigorous control and containment. The idea of a 'green belt' surrounding all major cities, of planned and zoned development separating industry from residential areas, and of adequate traffic management with arterial roads leading straight from the city centres were all current ideas by the eve of the Second World War. In 1935, for example, Sir Ernest Simon looked forward to the large-scale reconstruction of much of the southern half of the city of Manchester, including the city centre. There remained 80,000 slum houses to be demolished, to be replaced by modern houses or flats. This would provide a 'splendid opportunity', he believed, for replanning the central area on the best modern lines, and for making a comprehensive plan for a unified scheme of redevelopment. This was the authentic voice of the modern planner, and already in the 1930s, the essential features were there: the appeal to the best modern practice seen elsewhere – Simon was a great admirer of the better-planned German cities – and sweeping, grandiose redevelopment in accordance with a plan.[11]

'Planning' was now the vogue word and it is clear that for many planning represented the fusion of the still vital forces of optimism and social concern inherited from the past with the scientific and technocratic spirit of the twentieth century. It was, too, characterised by its faith in experts and 'the best modern practice', a certain highmindness, and a distinct sense of what was best for other people. But although plans proliferated in the years up to the Second World War, governments and local authorities had neither the resources nor the will to carry out redevelopment on the scale envisaged by some of the architects and town planners.

The Second World War broke this impasse. The destruction of thousands of acres of property in the blitz turned the 'rebuilding of Britain' from a vaguely desirable ideal into a practical necessity. Hardly had the dust settled on the bomb damage when ambitious schemes for large-scale rebuilding were pouring off the drawing boards of architects and planners. The government provided encouragement, for just as in the First World War, the theme of a new Britain arising from the rubble was a powerful weapon in maintaining civilian morale. In October 1940, Sir John Reith was appointed Minister of Works, not only to supervise the repair of bomb damage, but also to supervise plans for rebuilding the cities. The result was a series of plans commissioned from some of the most eminent pre-war architects and planners for rebuilding bombed cities such as Glasgow, Exeter, Hull and Coventry.[12] Coventry, one of the most rapidly growing towns of the inter-war years, had set up an architects' department as early as 1938 and begun plans to remodel the city centre. But its plans remained just that until the dramatic air-raids of November 1940 destroyed a large part of the city centre. Coventry was chosen as one of the cities in which Reith sought to instil a hope

4.8. Bomb damage in
Coventry

4.9. The choice for the
future

for the future by offering a prospect of comprehensive planning and rebuilding. Within a few weeks of the blitz which had torn the centre out of the medieval city, sketches and plans were being prepared for a redesigned city centre based upon pedestrianised shopping precincts, an inner ring road and zoned development in the suburbs.[13] Town planning was the symbolic standard-bearer for a new future for all. The planning, which was widely seen as essential to Britain's war effort in terms of the deployment and use of manpower and resources, was now to be turned to the creation of a better world when peace came. In *Picture Post* in January 1941, Maxwell Fry summed it up with the phrase 'The new Britain must be planned': plans were required for industry, housing, schools, hospitals and transport; plans would bring green grass to the towns and the amenities of the town to the village.

The Second World War gave an enormous credibility to planning and to a trust in experts who would do the best for the people. Architects and town planners wove ambitious schemes which were to find their expression in the post-war years. Some were entirely beneficial. Tougher controls over land-use and development attempted to halt the inexorable drift of industry and housing to the south-east. Better planning controls attempted to protect the countryside from speculative development and to regulate what was built. Green belts were established to provide a 'green lung' for the big cities. Amongst the most successful of the ideas given its head was that of the new towns, legislated for in 1947, and which ushered in on a grand scale the type of schemes pioneered at Letchworth, Welwyn and Wythenshawe before the Second World War. To foreigners, Britain's programme of new towns in the years after 1945, places such as Stevenage and Harlow, near London, and Peterlee in Scotland, were objects of admiration and emulation.[14] Rebuilt city centres, such as that of Coventry, may not have satisfied everybody but could hardly be regarded as disasters.

Less successful were the attempts to rehouse thousands of people in poorer houses for whom progress had been interrupted by the war or whose homes had been destroyed or damaged. Political demands for more housing and relatively full municipal and government coffers in the boom years of the 1950s and 1960s unleashed a massive spate of clearance and rebuilding. Large tracts of town centres were razed to build ring roads, shopping developments and new housing. Increasingly, the pressure on house-building was expressed in a preference for high-rise flats using new and untested techniques. For a time at least, local authorities and planners seemed to join in a headlong race to change the face of every town and city in the British Isles.[15] When the multistorey tower block and large-scale deck-access schemes became the symbol of the New Jerusalem it was obvious that all was not well.

But the malaise went somewhat deeper than ill-thought-out and poorly executed architectural schemes. There was a growing realisation that planning had not solved all the problems of modern society. Just as justifiable pride in the creation of the welfare state and the National Health Service gradually gave way to concern in the 1950s and 1960s that new and difficult problems had arisen, so there was increasing awareness that creating a better physical environment did not take into account the more intangible factors which went to make up a satisfactory community. There had already been signs of insensitivity to popular feeling in some of the pre-war estates and a lack of appreciation of what could happen when with the best of intentions whole communities were demolished and relocated in new estates. Too often in the post-war years, planners and architects were encouraged by both local and national politicians to rush pell-mell into putting roofs over people's heads in order to solve a pressing housing crisis, without consulting those for whom the dwellings were being built. The concern was still overwhelmingly with providing the physical amenities − more space, inside toilets and bathrooms, sufficient bedrooms for a whole family − that were so conspicuously lacking in the older housing. But while the creators of the new housing had available to them objective measures of floor space per person and overcrowding standards, they had no criteria for the less obvious factors − neighbourliness, a sense of safety and security, and the psychological and aesthetic qualities of much new housing. The vast expansion of some of the pre-war estates in the post-war years, in places such as Kirkby, near Liverpool, intensified problems that had already been identified, while some of the green-field housing estates seemed only to breed greater problems, not less. Lack of amenities and the bleak monotony of the estates began to raise new concerns about vandalism, crime and loneliness, especially amongst the elderly. Even the houseproud found it difficult to stop the appearance of graffiti and the development of a general air of scruffiness on some of the new estates, where children and young people ran wild and there was less sense of communal responsibility for what went on beyond people's front doors. It began to be remarked upon that people who had once polished the front step and sat at the front door in good weather where they could keep an eye on what went on in their street, left doors unlocked and 'popped in and out of neighbours' houses, were increasingly turning in on themselves, locking the doors of their new houses and flats against a scruffy, unruly world outside.

And in general the British proved reluctant flatdwellers. Continental cities with their different civic culture and long tradition of flatdwelling proved a poor model for British conditions and social habits. Instead of developing communal facilities to integrate the inhabitants, the new blocks were too often seen by their inhabitants for what they were, immense human warrens which paid little regard to how people actually wanted to live. Young parents found it impossible to supervise young children at play from several storeys up; passage ways and stairwells fell prey to litter and graffiti, while the sense of crowded multioccupancy accorded little with aspirations for a better life. Even if all the new tower blocks and deck-access flats had been well designed and soundly constructed – and many were not, with notorious difficulties over heating, damp, and poor materials – there was a profound sense in which the advocates of rehousing and slum clearance had overestimated their ability to reshape people's lives. In Sheffield, for example, one of the most ambitious schemes was that to replace the slum district of Parkhill with flats. There were ambitious ideas of replacing the old terraced streets on their grid-iron layout with 'streets in the sky', vertical communities replacing the wasteful, horizontal development and taking advantage of modern

4.10. The construction of the Parkhill Flats

industrialised building methods. But however imaginative, such schemes found it difficult to overcome an air of mass production and crude social engineering.

Such disillusion occurred at a time when post-war writers and social investigators were beginning to appreciate some of the more intangible features of the very communities which were being cleared during the post-war decades. Studies of older communities, like the East End of London, documented the closely-knit, supportive networks which made life tolerable and even enjoyable in spite of the often depressing physical environment.[16] Seebohm Rowntree also lived long enough to reflect ruefully in his study of *English Life and Leisure* in the early 1950s that human progress was not inevitably onwards and upwards; regrettably, not everyone wanted to spend their time in the New Jerusalem tending their gardens and inhabiting a drink-free zone.[17] A greater appreciation of people's wants, as opposed to their needs, and a little more awareness of life as it was lived sat uneasily with much of the redevelopment which was taking place in post-war Britain. It was, arguably, symptomatic that one of the most popular television series of the 1950s and 1960s, *Coronation Street*, was a deliberate evocation of the cosy, run-down urban communities which councils up and down the country were systematically demolishing in their thousands.

The collapse of part of the Ronan Point tower block in London in 1968, following a gas explosion, was one of those chance happenings which become symbolic of a whole era and mood. Behind the subsequent narrow concern with the safety of tower blocks built with some of the new techniques lay a much more generalised disquiet. It tapped a great reservoir of dissatisfaction with the new world created by architects, planners and politicians. The headlong rush to build a better world seemed to have run up against not just a minor technical hitch, but a host of far more complex and deep-seated problems than originally envisaged.[18] It was becoming apparent that the New Jerusalem could not be created in bricks and mortar alone, still less in prefabricated concrete and breeze-block modernism. The long-standing faith in progress and improvement through rational intervention on the part of the less fortunate was threatened with a complete breakdown. Trust in experts, in the best 'modern practice', was rapidly discounted by the experience of the reality of life in their creations. By the late 1970s, not only had the money for wholesale redevelopment dried up, but faith had been lost. Following the example of the United States, recently erected blocks of flats which had proved unlivable in were either demolished or sold off for refurbishment by private developers. Tower block was a dirty word and modern architecture a phrase unfit for decent company. Town and city plans lay abandoned and unfinished, along with ring roads that stopped abruptly and urban motorways which led nowhere. And yet it was not all waste. There were good estates, many built on traditional lines; the new towns were largely a success; planning had limited the worst excesses of unregulated urban sprawl, and the 'green belts' were seen as a success and something to be protected. Moreover, there were important lessons learned about the need for consultation and participation by those involved in redevelopment and new housing schemes. Planning, the vogue word of wartime and post-war social policy, increasingly yielded to community and neighbourhood as the starting point for any new scheme. The negative experience of what apparent experts could do also gave greater confidence to individuals and groups of people in their attempts to control their own environment. The most important legacy of some of the appalling mistakes made in the name of progress was a much greater sensitivity to the desires and aspirations of those who were its intended beneficiaries.

Further Reading

P. Addison, *The Road to 1945: British Politics and the Second World War* (London, 1975); J. Burnett, *A Social History of Housing, 1815–1970* (London, 1980); P. Keating, *Into Unknown England, 1866–1913* (London, 1976); A. Marwick, *British Society since 1945* (Harmondsworth, 1982); A. Quiney, *House and Home* (London, 1986); J. Stevenson, *British Society, 1914–45* (Harmondsworth, 1984).

CHAPTER FIVE

A Woman's Place

Pat Thane

To begin with the biographies of four women. The first was born in 1888, the daughter of a farm labourer in Cheshire. She was good at school and, unlike her own mother and generations of women before her, she was actually given a systematic education, though there was no question of her staying on beyond the age of 13. Then she followed her mother into service, at Eaton Hall, the nearby great house of the Duke of Westminster. She stayed there until she married a farm labourer, then had two children, a girl and a boy. Both were difficult births which permanently impaired her health. Her husband died in the 'flu epidemic which followed the First World War. To support her children, before there was a welfare state, she left them with her sister-in-law in Chester, while she returned to service, as housekeeper to a pawnbroker in Birkenhead. She remarried, an intermittently un-employed boilermaker, battled to keep house in the bug-ridden terraces of Merseyside in the 1930s and late in life had another child, who died in infancy. Always busy, always resilient; respectable, always poor, she died in a council flat in Birkenhead in the 1950s.

The second woman, her daughter, was raised in her aunt's terraced house in the inter-war years. Benefiting from an improved education system, somewhat wider opportunities for girls and the support of her mother and aunt, she trained as a typist; her brother became a farm labourer, like his father. She married a flight officer in the RAF and during the war had a daughter, who was cared for by her grandmother while she herself continued to work in an office. Her husband was killed. She carried on working until she too remarried. Thereafter she had four more children and devoted herself to caring for them and an increasingly sick and dependent husband.

The third woman, her daughter, was brought up by her grand-parents after her mother's remarriage. As one of the first generation to benefit from the 1944 Education Act, she was the first of the family to go to university, to Oxford, although there is no reason to believe that she was cleverer than the women who had gone before her. She became a university teacher, married and had a daughter of her own, without giving up work. She is now no longer married and is the first of these women whose marriage has been ended by choice rather than by the death of a husband. She is the first to have chosen to combine work and motherhood, rather than having the choice imposed on her by circumstances she could not control; the first to have raised her daughter without help from female relatives, and to have been able to afford paid help.

The fourth woman is her daughter, born in 1967. She has grown up at a level of comfort and with expectations both material and concerning possibilities for women which her predecessors could hardly imagine. Now at university, she expects to have children and a career but her future remains, of course, to be seen.

These are the stories of, respectively, my grandmother, my mother, myself and my daughter. Four women whose lives span a century and embody important features of the tension between continuity and change which characterises women's experience over that time.

More women have had access to education and hence the chance to be upwardly socially mobile by their own efforts, rather than through inheritance or marriage. A gradually wider range of jobs has opened up to more of them, beginning with the white-collar secretarial, clerical and teaching jobs at the end of the nineteenth century; more recently those giving access to real power – in the law, in banking, the civil service, as prime minister – for a very few, but still in numbers never known before. More women married and unmarried, with or without children, in all social classes, can lead relatively independent lives, unshackled by conventions which prescribe radically different social norms for men and women, than at any past time. Over the century women have, at least in principle, acquired equal access with men to divorce, equal rights to control their own income and property, equal rights to vote and to stand for election. This is all well known, but it is worth reminding ourselves, for all the inequalities that remain, how recent and how entirely new historically have been the moves towards greater equality in the experiences of men and women.

The four biographies also suggest what has not changed. Above all, society's expectation that domestic responsibilities for housekeeping and childrearing are primarily the woman's, no matter what else she may do; and the ambiguity of the response of most women to this expectation. None of these four women has accepted domesticity as her sole role, but neither has any of us rejected or been hostile to it as an important part of our lives. It is the way that women have combined domestic and public roles over the past century, and its significance, that is my main theme.

The nature of the domestic role itself has changed – most dramatically concerning marriage and childbirth. Over the past century the birth rate has fallen faster than at any time in history. The average woman marrying around 1890 experienced 10 pregnancies and spent 15 years either pregnant or nursing.[1] Now the average is around four years. The gradual spread of effective techniques of contraception has given women a wholly new sense of control over their own lives and a longer span of life free from pregnancy and child care. Most women now complete their families in their early 30s, whereas up to the Second World War they had their last child in their late 30s or 40s.

They are also in better health to enjoy their greater freedom, due as much to improved living standrds as to improvements in medicine. As late as 1939, Margery Spring-Rice's survey, *Working Class Wives*,[2] discovered many women such as:

Mrs A. of Birmingham [who] is 30, has been married twelve years, and had ten children. She suffers from 'swollen legs and veins' and a 'great weariness and headaches'. She has been advised to go into hospital and rest for the first and to have her eyes tested and to have more fresh air. She cannot manage any of these remedies due to poverty and family responsibility.

Full employment and higher living standards after the war, together with the introduction of the National Health Service in 1948, brought incalculable gains for women's health.

At the same time many more women have married and had children. A hundred years ago, about 15 in 100 women did not marry. This was partly because there was a majority of females in the population, long before the slaughter of men in the First World War. In fact, beginning around the First World War, marriage rates have risen. Of women born around 1940 only 5 in 100 have not married at least once. And fewer married women are childless than at any time up to the Second World War. So though familes have become smaller, they have also become more numerous.

Marriage itself has changed, above all becoming a potentially lengthier commitment. High adult death rates a century ago meant that there was a high chance of a marriage being broken in middle age, by death. Now, with longer life expectancy, a couple marrying in their 20s can contemplate spending up to 50 years together. The growth of divorce should be seen against this background. When marriages can last so long, it is not surprising that they face more strains. In fact the proportion of marriages broken by divorce in middle life at present is almost identical to the number broken by death a hundred years ago. It looks as though very long marriages are, in fact, difficult for many people to sustain. The proportion of female-headed, single-parent families is also similar to a century ago – the cause then was widowhood; now it is separation.[3]

There was a brief period, from the inter-war years to the 1950s, when long, stable marriages were more common. This was a period when life expectancy had lengthened and divorce was difficult to obtain and still socially unacceptable. It was then that our image of the normal marriage seems to have been fixed; however, it was a transient phenomenon. In this, as in other ways, the middle decades of the twentieth century were historically unusual, above all in their social stability, and we appear to be returning now to longer established patterns of behaviour.

These fundamental facts of life and death have profoundly altered women's and men's experiences. So also have economic and technological changes affecting, for example, housework. At the beginning of this century the bulk of poorer women lived in cramped households, without running water, with only the most basic facilities for cooking. Even for the better-off, middle-class housewife, running a complex household including several children or servants, with limited domestic equipment, was a time-consuming task which left little time for leisure. The popular image of the idle Victorian lady of the house, when it was any more than an ideal, was a reality for, at best, a small minority of the upper and upper-middle class.[4]

In the inter-war years, the boom in building council and private housing brought better kitchens, running water, bathrooms and gardens to more families. Indeed, our image of domestic normality owes a great deal to the picture of the suburban house and garden promoted by the expanding advertising and film industries of the 1930s. But still in 1939 Margery Spring-Rice described:

poor houses, but not slums . . . but every possible drawback exists to make her work hard and less pleasant . . . living on an upper floor, she has probably to carry her clean water upstairs from the basement, or at best from a tap on a midway landing and carry it down again to be emptied. She may have to heat it on an open fire in a room which has no cooking stove; there may possibly be a gas ring. The baby's pram will have to be hauled up and down stairs so that it does not clutter up the dark and gloomy hall. There is no possibility of an outside larder or a decent cupboard in which to keep food; coal has to be stored in the sitting-room. The w.c. may be three flights down . . . is shared by all the tenants of the house and has to be kept clean by each tenant in turn. There is no privacy whatsoever; other people's noise, the smell of other people's cooking, the continual passing of other people's footsteps.

These were conditions from which many, like my grandparents, did not escape until the next council house building boom, in the 1950s. Since the 1950s also, most women have benefited from the availability of improved cookers, vacuum cleaners, washing machines and so on. It has not, however, reduced the hours spent on housework, which have hardly changed over the century. Rather, standards and expectations have risen. People own more clothing and other possessions and they demand higher levels of cleanliness.

But women's lives have not been bounded by family and home, powerfully though they have been structured by their domestic obligations. Throughout the century very many women, from all types of background, have been active outside the home. This has partly been due to poverty. A hundred years ago many, perhaps most, manual workers brought home incomes so low and irregular that married women had to be continually on the lookout for ways to supplement them, and their unmarried daughters would certainly work. In fact the pattern for married women was often the reverse of that expected today. Mothers were most likely to go out to work when their children were young and the family had most mouths to feed and the lowest income, giving up the double burden, with relief, when the children were old enough to earn. Liberation for these women meant *escape* from the double toil of housework and paid work in late-Victorian conditions. We have seen how serious poverty persisted to the beginning of the Second World War and, in the 1980s, high levels of male unemployment give many wives little choice about whether or not they go out to work.[5]

But at all times women in all classes have worked from choice as well as necessity, for the independence it gave them. As a working woman told the social investigator, Clementina Black, in 1904: 'A shilling of your own is worth *two* that he gives you!'[6] At various times women of all backgrounds have faced pressure or encouragement to join the labour market. They have in fact faced conflicting exhortations from influential sources at different times over the century.

In the later nineteenth century and up to the First World War, the stable home and the good mother were seen as the key to rearing the strong, healthy and stable population needed to build and defend the British Empire against competition and ultimately war with other countries. In an almost mystical sense women were described as embodying the essence of what made and kept Britain Great; it was their duty to transmit it to future generations and to nurture it in their homes. In 1914, Dr Elizabeth Sloan Chesser, in *From Girlhood to Womanhood*, a widely read manual, declared that:

> Every girl has a duty to the race. . . . For she is the vase of life; she has in her body the power of handing on and on the life-force which has come to her through millions of years. It is a very sacred and serious thought – is it not? – that your life is so vital a matter to others yet unborn, that by your conduct you can help to keep the life-stream pure, help to uplift the race.[7]

It was at this time that domesticity as women's sole role came closest to fulfilment, in the late-Victorian middle class. But at the same time women from this very background sought a wider role. Middle-class wives devoted a large amount of time to voluntary charitable work and were active in public campaigns of all kinds, from temperance to Votes for Women. Such activities were a serious commitment, often

5.1. Women at work; a tailoring shop, 1908

5.2. Middle-class
women visiting slum
dwellers, 1912

fuelled by religious conviction, not the mere dilettantism of under-employed women which is often assumed. Such activities can be seen as the forerunners of female involvement in social work and pressure group activity in more recent times.[8]

What it was socially acceptable for them to do in public was limited, but even the limits were under constant scrutiny. It is a shock to our stereotypes of Victorian expectations of women to read in the, even then, very respectable *Daily Telegraph* in 1888 a leader asserting:

> The idea that a woman is born either to lounge through life as a lady or to drudge through it as a poor man's wife with, in both cases, narrowed domestic interests is a superstition having its origins in the east. Women have souls and aspirations of their own and if . . . they possess personal talents or tastes we see nothing to object to in their entry into a fair and free labour market.

For two weeks letters poured into the *Telegraph* in response, from men and women expressing almost every imaginable view on the subject. But surprisingly typical was that from a 'City merchant' from

Tufnell Park, London, who claimed to have employed women as clerks in his office for years:

> if the movement of women working for themselves goes forward, as all true men wish, thousands of women will be far too enlightened and circumstances will not make it necessary for them to rush into the ties of matrimony without due consideration ... let mothers bring up their daughters to think it lowering to their womanhood to look upon matrimony as the 'one thing needful', that if they have not a dependancy they must work ... are there no fathers who repent the day they saw their daughters marry? And how often do we not hear married women advise their sisters to 'keep as they are'? If a woman can marry a worthy man, by all means let her do so, but with a profession or trade behind her she can look before she leaps.[9]

5.3. The arrest of a suffragette

5.4. Recruiting poster, First World War

5.5. Recruiting poster, Second World War

Such sentiments were not unusual, but were part of a wider public debate which continued up to the First World War, and beyond, about the role of women in society and in particular the relatively greater constraints that marriage and the divorce laws imposed upon them compared with men.[10]

When war came, in 1914, women were urged that their duty to the nation lay in entering the workforce and they were admitted to some occupations, such as the armed services (in ancillary roles, as clerks and drivers) for the first time. In fact, contrary to popular belief, rather few women who had not previously worked entered the labour force. Few of them took over male jobs and even fewer held onto such jobs after the war – and those who did were more often white-collar than manual workers. Many middle-class girls were permanently socially liberated by the war.[11] In the 1920s the 'flapper' took the place of the chaperoned young lady of the 1890s. For working-class women much less changed; and throughout the war all women were

5.6. Women making munitions, First World War

urged to be mothers as well as workers. Government propaganda urged women to have babies to replace the thousands dead in the trenches. This reached a peak in National Baby week in July 1917. The Bishop of Fulham announced, 'While nine soldiers died every hour in 1915, twelve babies died every hour', so it was more dangerous to be a baby than a soldier.[12]

After the war, and still more during the depression, women were encouraged to remain at home to liberate jobs for men, though simultaneously the economy created new factory jobs for women, (producing light electrical goods for example). In the Second World War they were once more in demand for war production and war service, though fears of population decline due to the persistently declining birth rate meant that motherhood still had high priority.[13] Once more when the war was over women were expected to return to the home.[14] But, by the end of the 1940s, a labour shortage was unexpectedly apparent and the Ministry of Labour was encouraging

5.7. Cooking at an open range, London, 1940

women to return to the workforce at least part-time. In large numbers they did, and have remained.[15] The 1980s have once more seen a conflict between government statements on the vital contribution of home and family to social stability and economic policies designed to attract women into low-paid, part-time work.

So, contrary to what is often asserted, over the century women have not received unambiguous conditioning into domesticity. There has, however, been little change in the assumption that women carry the *primary* domestic responsibility in any household, even though they may also be in full-time work. We can find influential statements of how women should regard their primary role at any point in the century, sometimes in surprising places. D.W. Winnicott's *The Child, The Family and the Outside World*, a best selling baby-care manual of the 1960s, first prepared as successful radio talks, and read avidly by progressive mothers, suggests that it could be:

> agreed perhaps without anything actually being said, that the wife runs her home her way while the man has his own way at work. Everyone knows that an Englishman's home is his wife's castle. And in his home a man likes to see his wife in charge, identified with the home.[16]

The belief that the male role in the household is essentially only supportive and ancillary has been equally consistent over the century.

The absence of change in dominant perceptions of the male role has necessarily held back change in the expected role of women. And in the world of paid work women have received only limited encouragement to rise above low-paid, low-status jobs.

But it would be quite wrong to think of women as passive victims, largely accepting a subordinate position in society, imposed by others. It was, as already pointed out, the very group to whom the domestic ideal was preached most vigorously, the women of the Victorian middle class, who led the first effective demands for better education, wider job opportunities, legal equality and the vote; above all, for independence.[17] And working-class women have since the nineteenth century been more assertive than is often assumed. Their role in political movements, including the formation of the Labour Party, is underestimated as is their willingness to be involved in industrial militancy. Though it is often assumed that women are politically more conservative than men, there is little clear supporting evidence. Working women have been at least as likely as men in comparable, low-status occupations to unionise and, once in unions, they are rather more likely than male workers to stand up for their rights by a variety of means including striking, and to do so with considerable persistence. Also, contrary to another myth, women have a long history of active support for the industrial disputes of their menfolk. When in Crewe, in the 1870s, men were unfairly dismissed from the railway works, the wives of workers turned out in protest, because, unlike their husbands, they could not be identified and sacked. The

5.8. Women among coal strikers in the Bolton area, 1912

support of the wives in the miners' strike of 1985 was not something new but an episode in a much longer tradition.

A self-conscious women's movement has had an intermittent existence over the past century. It was strongest before the First World War and in the 1970s. In both phases, it involved only a minority of women. But more women have been more persistently and continuously involved in pushing back the grosser forms of inequality separating their experiences from those of males in a variety of campaigns on individual issues. For example, notably large numbers of women of varied backgrounds demonstrated in support of abortion reform in the 1970s. In less dramatic ways, the influence of the modern women's movement has been more pervasive than the popular press would have us think, though less than committed feminists would wish. Equal opportunities legislation has brought about a significant narrowing of pay differentials between men and women over the past decade.

Over the past century women's lives have changed in the direction of greater independence for more of them, though the changes have been incomplete and ambiguous. For example, in the 1890s, the first issues of the *Daily Mirror* spoke for the rights of women; in the 1980s it gives more space to 'Page Three Girls'. More women have more freedom and power than before; yet many are hardly more liberated than a century ago. Neither, of course, are many men. This is partly because a change as fundamental as altering the age-old relationship between the sexes is likely to be slow. And bringing about change has

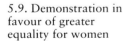

5.9. Demonstration in favour of greater equality for women

proved more difficult than the early feminists expected, partly due to demographic and economic changes which were unforseeable and beyond women's direct control.

They did not expect a higher proportion of women to become mothers as time went on, or that divorce and separation would leave so many on their own to care for children. Above all, they overestimated the ease with which centuries of conditioning of males and females into conventional roles could be modified. It is partly because change in women's lives and opportunities requires change also in those of men. This has not been forthcoming to any great extent, particularly in the direction of greater sharing of domestic roles.

We must also recognise that women's own ambitions have been conflicting and ambiguous. If we are to measure what women have gained over the past century, to some degree the yardstick must be their own expressed ambitions. A minority has aimed for more or less equal lives with men. Another minority has opted for domesticity. But more have sought freedom to choose to combine domestic and public roles in the ways that suit their lives, which will vary from person to person and at different points in the life cycle. In reality, women have been as reluctant to abandon a substantial commitment to domesticity as they have been to accept total immersion in it. This cannot only be explained by conditioning, which has been, as we have seen, ambiguous in its thrust. Perhaps it is because childrearing in particular is at least as fulfilling as any other activity and more so than most. Perhaps also, it is because domesticity gives women their one historic source of power over themselves and others and we are thus reluctant to give it up. If women have not yet achieved equal opportunities with men it is partly because a great deal has been and is stacked against us; but perhaps it is also because we are not wholly convinced that everything in the lives of men is so enviable.

Further Reading

Angela John (ed.), *Unequal Opportunities. Women's Employment in England 1800–1918* (Oxford, 1986); Jane Lewis, *Women in England 1870–1950* (Brighton, 1984); Jane Lewis (ed.), *Labour and Love. Women's Experience of Home and Family 1850–1918* (Oxford, 1986); Jill Liddington and Jill Norris, *One Hand Tied Behind Us. The Rise of the Women's Suffrage Movement* (London, 1978); Elizabeth Roberts, *A Woman's Place. An Oral History of Working Class Women 1890–1940* (Oxford, 1984); Pat Thane, 'Late Victorian Women' in T.G. Gourvish and A. O'Day (eds), *Later Victorian Britain* (London, 1988); Martha Vicinus, *Independent Women. Work and Community for Single Women 1850–1920* (London, 1985).

In Place of Fear

Adrian Wooldridge

Over the last decade the welfare state has aroused vigorous opposition. Its critics argue that it is extravagantly expensive and extremely inefficient. They suggest that it provides inferior services in return for compulsory contributions. They complain that it weakens the spirit of enterprise by penalising the successful with taxation and rewarding the indolent with benefits. At the same time patients and welfare claimants complain about slow, inefficient and often rude service. Once almost above criticism, the British welfare state is now a subject of controversy. 'Amidst our well publicized difficulties', Margaret Thatcher has argued, 'a vital new debate is beginning, or perhaps an old debate is being renewed, about the proper role of government, the welfare state and the attitudes on which it rests.'[1]

Paradoxically, this 'vital new debate' has probably favoured the left rather than the right. In the last election campaign the Labour leader, Neil Kinnock, made valuable political capital out of the welfare state; and he skilfully used historical arguments to reinforce his political polemic. He argued that the welfare state embodies a commitment to a just and compassionate society, based on cooperation and dedicated to the common good; that the Labour Party promises to uphold the welfare state while the Conservative Party threatens to undermine it, substituting the values of the marketplace for those of the neighbourhood; and that the last seven years of Conservative government have already brought a dramatic weakening of England's welfare services. During the post-war years, he argued, all three political parties agreed to sink their political differences when it came to welfare. But Margaret Thatcher has undermined this consensus and is threatening to dismantle the welfare state. Paradoxically, as far as the welfare state is concerned, the Labour Party is posing as the party of conservatism and branding the Tories as dangerous radicals.

Neil Kinnock's version of the history of the welfare state is attractive. Unfortunately, it is not entirely accurate. The founders of the welfare state espoused ideas which might shock Mr Kinnock. Britain's commitment to welfare has always been somewhat hesitant, and viewed in the long term, Mrs Thatcher's opinions are rather conventional. In practice, the welfare state has dramatically failed to promote equality, as Mr Kinnock implies. Instead, it may well have done as much to subsidise the middle classes as to support the unfortunate.

It is perhaps worth beginning by asking a simple but rather tricky question: what is a welfare state? Put simply, the phrase denotes a state in which organised national power is deliberately used in order to modify the play of market forces in three main directions: first, to guarantee individuals and families a minimum income irrespective of the market value of their work or property; second, to minimise personal insecurity by enabling individuals and families to meet 'social contingencies' – notably sickness, old age and unemployment – which would otherwise lead to disaster; and third, to ensure that all citizens, regardless of status and class, are provided with certain social services, such as education.[2] The welfare state is the antithesis of the liberal or, as some call it, the *laissez-faire* state, which refuses to intervene in the economy, emphasises self-help rather than collective provision, and insists that social services should be provided by the market, through private medical insurance or private pension schemes – or not at all.

The phrase 'welfare state' was first used to describe Labour Britain after 1945. But the decisive break between the *laissez-faire* and the welfare state was made not by the Labour government of 1945–51 but by the Liberal governments of 1905–14. In an unprecedented burst of legislative activity, the Liberals introduced free school meals for needy children in 1906, medical inspection of state school children in 1907, old age pensions in 1908, a 'budget against poverty' in 1909 and national insurance schemes against ill health and unemployment in 1911. This legislation embodied a radically new development – the taxation of the entire population to provide benefits for the unfortunate and the removal of the poor law stigma from social welfare.[3] The Victorians had insisted that paupers should be stigmatised in order to discourage idleness and provide incentives to work and save: in consequence they deprived them of the vote and consigned them to semi-penal conditions in the poorhouse. The Liberals began to remove the stigma from pauperism and to provide relief as a popular right.

This early welfare legislation was largely inspired by issues of national power and imperial politics.[4] It was a tool of national efficiency rather than a register of national compassion. In the late nineteenth century many commentators sensed that the sun was setting on the British Empire. The unification of Germany and the rise of the giant states – Russia and America – threatened Britain's international position. The British economy began to weaken: between 1883 and 1913, for example, its share of world trade in manufactured goods dropped from 37 to 25 per cent, and commentators predicted that its share would continue to decline (although even the most pessimistic would be surprised to discover just how far that decline has gone today). Britain's humiliation in the Boer War in

6.1. The Boer War

6.2. The Boer War

1899–1900 brought these mounting anxieties into focus. The revelation that almost half a million British and Colonial soldiers, backed up by massive military funds, had initially failed to crush a tiny nation of Afrikaners produced a surge of pessimism and introspection in the political nation. Many blamed this failure on the weakness of the British state, arguing that Britain should abandon its commitment to *laissez-faire* liberalism and model itself instead on its successful rival, Germany, with its powerful bureaucracy, its conscription, its tariffs and subsidies, and its welfare provisions.

Above all, the Boer War reinforced the fear that the quality of Britain's population – of its human stock in the language of the period – was deteriorating. Throughout the late nineteenth century government inquiries and independent social surveys had revealed details about the conditions of the mass of the population which shocked the comfortable classes and seemed to indicate long-term enfeeblement. The Boer War highlighted the physical unfitness of the inhabitants of the slums of Britain's large cities. In Manchester, for example, 8000 out of 11,000 volunteers were turned away as unfit. Such evidence seemed all the more worrying in the light of persistent reports that Germany was almost free from the undersized and unhealthy specimens who thronged in every large British town.

Not surprisingly, many people felt that the poor condition of the population meant disaster for the British Empire. The future Liberal prime minister, Lloyd George, warned that the nation would be unable

6.3. Kaiser Wilhelm II of Germany with his guard

to run an A1 empire equipped with only C3 health: 'The white man's burden had to be carried on strong backs'.[5] The earliest ventures in welfare provision were intended to remedy the problem of national deterioration and to create a healthy population capable of preserving a vigorous empire. The School Medical Service, which was both a precursor and a prototype of the National Health Service, was founded in 1907 in order to reverse the deterioration of the race and to improve the health of the future citizens of the empire. The provision of free school milk and free school meals, the establishment of compulsory medical inspection, and the founding of maternity and child welfare clinics were all inspired by a belief that 'the nation marches forward on the feet of the little children'.[6]

National interest was not the only reason for welfare legislation. The origins of the welfare state also owed something to idealism. From at least the late nineteenth century onwards, socialists and trade unionists argued that the state should intervene in the workings of the market to provide security for the unfortunate and opportunities for the poor; and that the working class should reorganise society on the basis of the satisfaction of common needs rather than the pursuit of private profit. The Fabians, a group of middle-class socialists led by Sidney and Beatrice Webb, were particularly influential in advocating social security legislation to provide 'an enforced minimum for civilized life'. Their arguments linked an extension in the claims made for citizenship with a re-evaluation of the social role of the state. Not surprisingly, the socialist case was powerfully reinforced by the extension of manhood suffrage in 1885.

Yet the thinkers who exercised most influence over the early welfare legislation were liberals rather than socialists. In the late nineteenth century liberal political thought underwent a revolution. Several influential intellectuals argued that liberals ought to abandon their commitment to a minimal 'night-watchman' state and instead encourage the state to intervene in the economy in order to promote common welfare. They also insisted that poverty owed more to social inequality than to personal immorality and that the poor should be helped rather than stigmatised. These arguments were rapidly converted into an orthodoxy: a new interventionist liberalism replaced the old *laissez-faire* liberalism.[7] Lord Milner noted this sea-change in contemporary thought:

> When I went up to Oxford [in the early 1870s] the *laissez faire* theory still held the field. All the recognized authorities were 'orthodox' economists of the old school. But within ten years the few men who still held the old doctrines in their extreme rigidity had come to be regarded as curiosities.[8]

6.4. The new
generation, 1901

6.5. An early school
meal

One of the most influential exponents of new liberalism was a tutor at Balliol College, Oxford, T.H. Green, who argued that the state ought to remove all obstacles to the development of social capacity, such as those arising from lack of education, poor health and bad housing. His doctrine of active state interference had a powerful influence on his pupils, who included many future policy-makers, most notably H.H. Asquith, the Liberal prime minister.[9] At the same time, Samuel Barnett's Settlement Movement encouraged privileged undergraduates to spend some time living and teaching among slumdwellers.[10] Perhaps for the first time in English history future civil servants and MPs had first-hand experience of the living conditions of the poor.

Yet these liberal reformers were more idealistic about the state than they were about the nation's poor. Brought up in the enclosed world of upper-middle-class England, and ensconced in privileged institutions such as Oxford and Cambridge colleges, they were ill-informed about the conditions which created and preserved poverty. Their experiences in slum-settlements did not always eradicate their class prejudices or instil a deep understanding of the causes of poverty. In general, they regretted suffering but never questioned the system that produced it. Many still inclined to explain social problems in terms of individual morality rather than social circumstances and consequently worried about the impact of social reforms on the characters of the poor. Their verdicts on their fellow citizens were often harsh. L.T. Hobhouse, a leading figure at the London School of Economics, argued that in an ideal society 'idleness would be regarded as a social pest, to be stamped out like crime',[11] and the young William Beveridge advocated 'complete and permanent loss of all citizenship rights' for the poor, through public institutions, emigration and even starvation. These attitudes were not confined to liberals. The Webbs regarded the 'reform of social conditions as a palliative for original sin'[12] and had little sympathy for the working class.[13] They advocated 'conditional relief', whereby those who received aid from society had to pay for it by improved behaviour: charity was an instrument of moral reform. Reformers thought of welfare in terms of state paternalism and administrative centralisation. Trained to rule, they habitually divided the world into those who did good and those to whom good was done. Their comfortable position in English established life and their links with the political elite dissuaded them from radical thought and encouraged a complacent belief in social engineering.

Some of the most important steps towards the formation of the British welfare state were taken in the unglamorous inter-war period – principally under Conservative governments. The political elite finally agreed that the state should support all its citizens at 'an enforced minimum for civilized life'; and economic depression and mass unemployment forced governments to intervene in the economy. The main obstacles to the nationalisation of social policy were swept aside. Traditional charitable assistance failed to deal with mass unemployment; the old Poor Law seemed increasingly unacceptable in theory and unworkable in practice; private insurers faced severe financial strains and were eager to off-load unprofitable risks onto the state; and professional groups were gradually co-opted into the national social security programme.[14] The state rapidly increased its capacity to spend money, employ service staff and subordinate local government. The number of social service employees doubled between 1914 and 1933 and quadrupled between 1933 and 1940, and between 1930 and 1950 about half of all public funds were spent on social services.

At the same time, the left gained valuable experience and generated influential ideas. The Labour Party learned to work within the parliamentary system, acquired policy-making experience, and began to see how social legislation could be used to advance its political aims. Left-wing intellectuals sat on official and semi-official government committees and helped to draft documents which both planned and popularised an expansion of the welfare services. In particular, the Board of Education's Consultative Committee, which included the socialist historian R.H. Tawney, issued a cycle of reports on every aspect of English education and laid the foundations of the 1944 Education Act.[15]

Despite these advances, Britain's commitment to welfare remained weak. Many people continued to be suspicious of welfare, feeling that it would encourage immorality and sap the will to work. Few politicians took a lively interest in welfare legislation: Churchill was not peculiar in preferring the champagne of grand strategy to the gruel of social legislation. The Labour Party was remarkably staid in its social thinking and its proposals for the relief of mass unemployment did little more than reiterate Edwardian recommendations. British trade unions took little part in social reforms. Their preoccupation with industrial conflicts distracted them from long-term consideration of the reform of the state, and union barons spent more time squabbling among themselves than they did thinking about social benefits. In particular, the Friendly Societies blunted Labour Party enthusiasm for social insurance and limited working-class involvement in new legislation. The Civil Service was responsible for the bulk of policy innovations, and the Treasury acquired enormous power over the social insurance system, playing a more direct role in shaping social policy than Finance Ministries in any other advanced country. In consequence, by 1939, Britain's welfare services were patchy, frugal, and infuriatingly complex.

The Second World War certainly gave an enormous impetus to the development of the British welfare state. The war strengthened demands for a more just and generous social order, administered by the state and devoted to popular welfare; a people which had endured common risks in the fight against Hitler deserved common securities in victory. In 1942 the *Beveridge Report*, the blue-print of the British welfare state, named 'five giant evils to be destroyed – Want, Disease, Ignorance, Squalor and Idleness'; and the intelligentsia applauded and extended these recommendations. Post-war legislation tried to embody these sentiments. The 1944 Education Act promised to make secondary education universal and to educate every child according to his 'age, ability and aptitude'; the National Insurance Act of 1946 guaranteed a safety-net for the unfortunate; and the National Health Act of 1948 laid the foundations for a free National Health Service. Aneurin Bevan summed up this legislation succinctly: 'homes, health, education and social security, these are your birthright'.

Support for the welfare state was not confined to the left. The three pillars of the welfare state – the Education Act, the National Insurance Act and the National Health Service Act – were associated with the names of Butler, Beveridge and Bevan, a Conservative, a Liberal and a Socialist. In 1949 a Conservative Party pamphlet, *The Right Road for Britain*, stated unequivocally that

> the social services are no longer even in theory a form of poor relief. They are a cooperative system of mutual aid and self-help provided by the whole nation and designed to give to all the basic minimum of security, of housing, of opportunity, of employment and of living standards below which our duty to one another forbids us to permit any one to fall.[16]

When the Conservatives won the election of October 1951 and R.A. Butler replaced Hugh Gaitskell as Chancellor of the Exchequer there was so little change in the direction of domestic policy that the term 'Butskellism' was coined to describe the phenomenon. Like warfare, welfare was above class politics.

But, even in this period of heady faith in social reconstruction, legislation was the work of hard-headed realists rather than soft-hearted idealists. During the war William Beveridge established almost autocratic control over the formation of welfare policy. He wanted to create a 'safety net' for the poor, not a more egalitarian society. His report, *Social Insurance and Allied Services*, proposed a system of compulsory insurance: in return for a single weekly flat rate contribution every contributor would receive benefits calculated to provide a minimum standard of living whenever his or her earnings were interrupted. It also encouraged people to provide more than the

6.6. A working-class family, Stoke-on-Trent, just after Second World War

minimum for themselves through voluntary action. When the post-war Labour government instituted National Insurance it was more generous than Beveridge. But even so the extent of the provision it envisaged was minimal compared with what exists today: the welfare state started life as a prop for the old at a time of full employment.

Beneath the generous rhetoric there remained a powerful current of class-conscious and even punitive sentiment. Some of the leading architects of the welfare state had little sympathy for the working class and felt in their bones that welfare beneficiaries were scroungers. Beveridge once commented to his brother-in-law, R.H. Tawney, that:

> The well-to-do represent on the whole a higher level of character and ability than the working classes, because in the course of time the better stocks have come to the top. A good stock is not permanently kept down: it forces its way up in the course of generations of social change, and so the upper classes are on the whole the better classes.[17]

He feared that welfare provision might weaken the incentive to work, encourage immorality and undermine voluntary assistance. He insisted that the unemployment pay should be conditional upon attendance at a work or training centre and he was prepared to leave the deserted mother or wife to public assistance.[18]

Even during the years of social reconstruction welfare legislation continued to be highly paternalistic. Welfare was the gift of one class to another rather than a common resource. Sympathy for the underdog was frequently vitiated by intellectual contempt. In *The Socialist Case*, Douglas Jay, one of the architects of Labour's post-war economic policy, argued that 'in the case of nutrition and health, just as in the case of education, the gentleman in Whitehall really does know better what is good for people than the people know themselves'.[19] Even the high priest of social welfare, Richard Titmuss, assumed that 'a small elite in a totally mobilized society could determine social and economic policies without the distractions, setbacks and inefficiencies of democratic governance'.[20]

In the event, even Beveridge's modest proposals were vigorously contested. Worried that increased taxes would extinguish economic growth, the Treasury lamented the loss of the Poor Law threat of prison for the unreformed unemployed and the ease of obtaining unemployment insurance, and objected to excessively high child benefits. In 1944 it estimated that all social spending in 1945 would be £450m, rising to £831m in 1965.[21] Popular enthusiasm for the *Beveridge Report* undermined Treasury influence but failed to convert policy-makers to a radical vision of future social policy. Even the National Health Service, the centrepiece of the British welfare state, was weakened by costly compromises with the medical establishment. Medical specialists and their teaching and research hospitals managed to insulate themselves from the national system. Family doctors preserved their professional autonomy and resisted proposals for health care centres, in which doctors were to work as a team and receive a salary in place of the traditional fee per individual patient.[22]

During the post-war economic boom the welfare state expanded enormously in its size and ambition. Yet it was much less successful at redistributing resources and solving social problems than many of its supporters had hoped. Four major criticisms can be levelled at the operation of the post-war welfare state.

First, the middle classes have done remarkably well out of the welfare state. Established to help the poor, it has often ended up by subsidising the affluent. The middle classes staff many of its departments and act as its most successful customers. They are assiduous in using its services and claiming its benefits. They are highly successful in the competition for scarce educational resources. As the number of educational opportunities increased so middle-class children came forward to claim them. The expansion of higher education in the 1960s produced subsidies for the affluent rather than opportunities for the poor, and the class composition of university students remains almost the same today as it was in the 1920s. Through student grants the state essentially subsidises middle-class people in their pursuit of middle-class jobs.

Indeed, the welfare state has often seemed to be more successful at providing jobs for administrators than services for the poor. In 1980 Britain employed over 5 million public servants, more than half as many again as France or West Germany. A great deal of medical expenditure seems to advance the interests of medical practitioners and scientists rather than patients. State-funded architecture and town planning often appear to be a conspiracy of professionals against the public. In particular, the high-rise flats, which became standard local authority products in the 1960s, were geared to the convenience of the crane and accountant rather than the tenant.[23] Despite its commendable aims, the practical impact of the welfare state has often been to support middle-class incomes and fuel middle-class aspirations.

Second, the welfare state has failed to eliminate many of the problems it was set up to tackle. Primary poverty persisted throughout the 1960s, particularly among one-parent families. R.H. Tawney's prediction that under a welfare state it 'would cease to be the rule for

6.7. The 'gentlemen in Whitehall'

the rich to be rewarded, not only with riches, but with a preferential share of health and life, and for the penalty of the poor to be not merely poverty, but ignorance, sickness and premature death'[24] has proved to be empty. Enormous inequalities persist in the health of the rich and the poor. In 1980 the risk of death before retirement was seven-and-a-half times as great for unskilled manual workers and their wives as for professional men and their wives. In 1980 a Department of Health and Social Security report, *Inequalities in Health* (known as the *Black Report* after its Chairman Sir Douglas Black) even argued that inequality in health has actually widened under the National Health Service.[25] The poor continue to do extremely badly in the race for educational qualifications. Comprehensive reorganisation and increased educational expenditure have done nothing to disrupt the connection between social background and educational success.[26]

Moreover, the welfare state has done remarkably little to reduce Britain's economic inequalities. In the early 1970s, the bottom 50 per cent of the population actually received less of the gross national income than it did in 1949. Progressive taxation has had little impact on the fortunes of the rich. The top 10 per cent still receive almost a quarter of post-tax income, only slightly less than they received in 1949. In 1972 the top 20 per cent of the population owned 85 per cent of all British wealth. The main post-war redistribution in wealth has not been between the rich and the poor but between the very rich and the rich.[27]

Third, the welfare state has imposed enormous burdens on the economy. Beveridge had estimated that there would be no real increase in the cost of health and rehabilitation services between 1945 and 1965, assuming that the welfare services would create a healthier nation. In fact spending rose astronomically.[28] By the mid 1970s almost half the nation's income was devoted to public expenditure, much of it to welfare. This has led to widespread reassessment of the relationship between public expenditure and economic growth. In the 1960s it was widely assumed that the social services were essential to a vigorous and sophisticated economy; in the 1970s many commentators presented them as antagonistic to growth, drawing resources from the productive sector of the economy, reducing incentives and curbing initiatives.[29] To many it seems that the untamed welfare state is capable of smothering the affluent society.

Fourth, the complexity of the welfare system has led to widespread dissatisfaction. A bewilderingly large number of benefits have been introduced by different government departments to support poor families. There are over a hundred DHSS leaflets on social security provision – and one of these is a leaflet that lists all the other leaflets. In consequence large numbers of eligible people fail to claim such entitlements as supplementary benefits, free school meals, rate rebates, rent allowances and free prescriptions. In 1979 only just over half of those eligible claimed rent allowances and free school meals.[30] 'Giant Complexity' should be added to Beveridge's Five Giant Evils.[31]

The welfare state, then, was not as Utopian in its origins, or as egalitarian in its impact, as Mr Kinnock imagines. On the other hand, its future is unlikely to be as dismal as he fears. The New Right mutters about dismantling the welfare state and extending the role of market forces; but in practice the Thatcher government is highly conventional in its approach to welfare: it tinkers but it does not demolish. Indeed, in 1987 the welfare state remains more generous and far more expensive than anything the Labour government of 1945 envisaged. The government has dramatically failed to fulfil its pledge to hold down public spending on welfare. Between 1979 and 1985 real spending rose by 1 per cent on education, 17 per cent on health and personal social services, and 28 per cent on social security.[32] In particular, the government has made no serious attempts to dismantle the National Health Service. Together with personal social services, the NHS absorbed almost 14 per cent of public expenditure in 1978–9. Its share is approximately 15 per cent today and heading for 16 per cent at the end of the decade. Furthermore, public commitment to the welfare state remains strong, particularly among the articulate middle class. Opinion polls indicate that the majority of the population wants to see more expenditure on services, even if it means higher taxation, and that very few people are willing to see services cut in return for lower taxation. The generosity of the boom years of the 1960s and early 1970s may be a thing of the past; but, unless something goes dramatically wrong with the British economy, the welfare state is here to stay.

Further Reading

Paul Addison, *The Road to 1945. British Politics and the Second World War* (London, 1977); Asa Briggs, 'The Welfare State in Historical Perspective', *The Collected Essays of Asa Briggs, Volume Two. Images, Problems, Standpoints, Forecasts* (Brighton, 1985), pp. 177–211; Bentley B. Gilbert, *The Evolution of National Insurance in Great Britain. The Origins of the Welfare State* (London, 1966); José Harris, *William Beveridge. A Biography* (Oxford, 1977); Malcolm Wicks, *A Future for All. Do We Need a Welfare State?* (Harmondsworth, 1987).

CHAPTER SEVEN

Mass Media, Mass Democracy

Paddy Scannell

Radio and television are so much a part of daily life for everyone today that it is hard to imagine a world without them. Yet broadcasting in this country is less than 70 years old. It began four years after the end of the Great War; four years after the Representation of the People Act in 1918 gave the vote to all adult males over 21 and all women over 30.[1] Mass political democracy and broadcasting are both quite recent things.[2] Their development is linked together in many ways. Both are particular to modern, twentieth-century life.

In the early 1920s strange, Heath Robinson contraptions began to appear in the gardens of Britain and on the rooftops of houses.[3] It was a common sight to see a forest of masts and turrets swaying high above suburban streets and avenues. A new craze was sweeping the country – listening-in to the wireless. In order to receive a programme it was necessary then to put up an aerial, usually about 100 feet long, suspended between two masts, either in the garden or on the roof. Failing that an elaborate catscradle device could be used indoors. The receiving equipment looked more like something out of science fiction than a simple household object. It took years before the design of the radio receiving apparatus settled into a recognisable standard set.

The first truly modern design was the celebrated Ekco set, produced by E.K. Cole's company.[4] Its shell was made from the most modern material, moulded bakelite. It had two knobs for wavelengths and tuning, and one for volume. The position of the major European stations was shown on the dial. It ran on mains electricity. It was the first, fully mass-produced cheap radio set and it created a sensation at

7.1. The Ecko set at Radiolympia, 1935

Radiolympia, the annual trade fair, in 1934. A year later the Phillips Company produced the Philco, the People's Set. It cost just over £5 and was designed to be within the purchase of any wage-earner. Its curved black bakelite case was reminiscent of the People's Car, the Volkswagon – which came into mass production in Germany at the same time.

By now the radio set was no longer a magical box that some technically minded male member of the household tinkered with in the garden shed, but an essential part of modern, domestic life. By 1939 there were 9 million radio licences taken out each year, representing 75 per cent of British households. For most people in the 1920s a wireless receiving set was probably the most ultra-modern device they had ever seen. By the end of the 1930s a radio in the living room or parlour was a taken-for-granted fixture; just part of the furniture.[5]

It was in this context that the broadcasters addressed their audience. Not as a mass audience, but as a nation of individuals, listening in the privacy of their homes, often as members of families. A special 'Listeners Own' number of *Radio Times* (15 April 1938) imagined the

7.2. The *Radio Times* issue featuring the *Listener Family*, 1938

7.3. The *Radio Times* Fireside number, 1935

radio audience as Mr and Mrs Listener with their four children and Fido the dog who also listened. 'All the family have different tastes', the leading article declared. 'So too that vastly greater family of listeners whom they symbolize.'

Radio, it was felt, might counter all the attractions of modern life outside the home and which, some argued, threatened to undermine it. The listening habit could restore a more rational use of leisure time and reinstate, as one commentator in *Radio Times* (2 May 1924) put it, 'the old love of home and family which has been such a bulwark against aggressions of all kinds for the British people'. The home was a retreat burrowed deeply away from the pressures of work and urban life. Thus a special 'Fireside Number' of *Radio Times* (15 November 1935) described the pleasures of privacy:

> To come home from work on a November evening through the wet confusion of the city, the humid press of bus or tram, the rain-dimmed streets that lead to the lights of your own home; to close the door behind you, with the curtains drawn against the rain, and the fire glowing in the hearth — that is one of the real pleasures of life. And it is when you are settled by your own fireside that you most appreciate the entertainment that broadcasting can bring.

The pleasures of listening developed by the BBC on the National Programme in the 1930s were designed to support the new and modest Utopia of the suburban nuclear family. The tired businessman or weary officeworker were models frequently invoked to typify the ordinary listener for whom relaxation after a hard working day or week was a well-earned right.[6]

What difference to people's daily life did the coming of broadcasting make? A prize-winning essay written in 1923 for a newspaper competition on 'What broadcasting has done for me', began:

> I live in a dull drab colliery village, as far removed from real country as from real city life — a bus ride from third rate entertainments and a considerable journey from any educational, musical or social advantages of a first class sort. In such an atmosphere life becomes rusty and apathetic. Into this monotony comes the introduction of a good radio set and my little world is transformed.[7]

An officer worker, writing to *Radio Times* (12 October 1928), declared:

I'm only writing to say how much radio means to me and thousands of the same sort. It is a real magic carpet. Before it was a fortnight at Rhyll, and that was all the travelling that I did that wasn't on a tram. Now I hear the Boat Race and the Derby, and the opening of the Menai Bridge. There are football matches some Saturdays, and talks by famous men and women who have travelled and can tell us about places.

For many, many people whose lives were bounded by a narrow routine, broadcasting brought access to the great public world beyond the immediate horizon. A survey conducted in 1939 into the impact of broadcasting on everyday life concluded that before radio conversation was largely restricted to humdrum and immediate things: the ups and downs of family life; the doings of neighbours; weddings, births and funerals in the district.[8] But now the wireless provided not merely a new way of passing time, but a new and vastly wider range of topics for discussion and debate amongst families and neighbours.

Modern society is characterised by the growing distance between the political and cultural centres of authority and power and the immediate daily environment of work and home. The real power of broadcasting came to lie in the way it straddled these two worlds of public and private life in a way no previous form of communication had been able to. From institutional centres it reached into the fabric

7.4. Family listening to the radio in 1931

7.5. John Reith

of ordinary daily life, touching peoples' lives with new resources of information, education and leisure. On the one hand it underpinned the pleasures of privacy. On the other, it provided outlets, mobility, access to the larger world beyond. This access was not won easily. In almost every case the broadcasters at first found themselves obstructed in their efforts to develop the full range of programmes that we all now take for granted.

John Reith was the first Director General of the BBC, and he played a key part in defining the development of broadcasting in this country as a public service. He was keenly aware, from the very beginning, of the political importance of radio in the new context of mass democracy. Many of those who now had the right to vote had had little formal education beyond the age of 14. The new medium of wireless might help in their political education as citizens of a modern democracy. In a book he wrote in 1924 he declared:

Broadcasting carries direct information on a hundred subjects to innumerable people. A new and mighty weight of public opinion is being formed, and an intelligent concern on many subjects will be manifested in quarters now overlooked. I have heard it argued that, insofar as broadcasting is awakening an interest in these hitherto more or less sheltered or inaccessible regions, it is fraught with danger to the community and the country generally. In other words I gather that it is urged that a state of ignorance is to be preferred to one of enlightenment. To disregard the spread of knowledge, with the consequent enlargement of opinion, and to be unable to supplement it with reasoned arguments, or to supply satisfactory answers to legitimate and intelligent questions, is not only dangerous but stupid.[9]

As Reith foresaw, public opinion is of crucial importance in mass democratic politics. If people are to exercise their political rights in an informed and reasonable way, they must have access to information about what those they have elected are doing on their behalf. And on top of that they must have access to open unconstrained debate on matters of general public concern. These two things — free access to news and discussion — constitute a fundamental citizenship right, 'the right to know'. They are the basis of an informed public opinion.

Broadcasting has always been crucial to this process because of the quite radically new kind of public that it created — a *general* public, the whole society. Before radio and television there simply was no means of communication that could speak directly to all members of society. There was no means of access for all to events as they happened. There was no means of instantly passing on news to all of political crises in the very moment of their unfolding. But broadcasting routinely and unremarkably does all these things. And for all these reasons those in power seek to control it to their own ends. For broadcasting not only gives the general public access to politics in a new and direct kind of way. It also gives politicians, parties and governments a new and direct access to this new general public.

The history of the development of news and political debate on radio and television is at least partly the history of the efforts of governments, parties, state departments and powerful interest groups to interfere with, censor or manipulate broadcast news and debate.[10] It is well known that the BBC sided with the government during the General Strike of 1926.[11] It had very little option. Governments have very real indirect powers over broadcasting and they have, over the years, behind the scenes threatened and cajoled the broadcasting authorities. Such pressures peak in moments of crisis — Munich in 1938, Suez in 1956, the Falklands War in 1982 — but they are a routine feature of the realities of life for staff responsible for news and politics on radio and television.[12]

The breaking of the BBC's monopoly in the 1950s certainly made broadcasting more resistant to such pressures. It is notable that it was commercial television which took the lead in developing most of the techniques of broadcast journalism that we are familiar with today. In particularly Independent Television News pioneered the use of filmed reports from the scene of the action, and the probing news interview. This was in sharp contrast to the unquestioning and deferential treatment of political issues by the BBC at the time. It is only in the last 30 years or so that politicians have – in news interviews and studio debates – been routinely called upon to answer for their actions to the listening and viewing publics.

One major consequence, then, of broadcasting has been to open up politics, making politicians directly answerable to the electorate for their conduct of the nation's affairs. It has helped to make political life more democratic. But in a more general way broadcasting has, in all sorts of ways, democratised culture, making it more public and available to the majority of people in ways previously not possible.

Consider music: before broadcasting only a tiny fraction of the population had ever heard a Beethoven symphony performed by a full-sized orchestra. Now, thanks to radio, everyone had access to such performances and the last step in the true democratisation of music could take place, as the BBC claimed in 1928:

7.6. Musicians recording in studio, 1923

The shepherd on the downs, or the lonely crofter in the farthest Hebrides and, what is equally important, the labourer in his squalid tenement in our but too familiar slums, or the lonely invalid on her monotonous couch, may all, in spirit, sit side by side with the patron of the stalls and hear some of the best performances in the world.[13]

Broadcasting has made good music universally available. And the same can be said of drama and the repertoire of classic British and European plays.

But we need to think on a broader scale than this narrow and, at times, patronising concept of culture. Broadcasting has extended public life by linking together and transforming a whole range of events and celebrations that had previously been fragmented and separate. Consider the Grand National, the Cup Final, a royal wedding, or the last night of the proms: all these events preceded radio and television. But each was available then only to the particular public that attended the occasion. Today the public world, in all its diversity, is familiar in ways that were simply impossible a century ago. Today every child, woman and man in this country knows the faces of royalty, political leaders or stars from the world of entertainment. Broadcasting has helped to normalise public life, down through the years, by continuously representing Britain as a *knowable* community, a community that is visible and accessible to all.[14]

At the same time a reverse process has been taking place whereby private life has been profoundly resocialised by radio and television. It has brought into the public domain the experiences and pleasures of the majority in ways that had hitherto been denied in the dominant traditions of literature and the arts.[15] In Shakespeare's day only those of gentle blood were suitable subjects for tragedy or romance. Rude mechanicals were subjects for knockabout farce. Since then, art and literature have increasingly dealt with the uneventful lives of the middling classes. By the end of the last century the working classes had become subjects for art and literature, but usually as objects of compassion or as social problems and always as described by middle-class authors for middle-class readers.

Broadcasting, first in radio and then in television, because its service was addressed to the whole of society, gradually came to represent the whole of society in its programmes. Today we are familiar with the idea of documentary programmes on major social issues such as poverty, unemployment or housing, in which the people who live in such conditions describe what it is like. Before the war such methods of presentation had actually to be invented. When, for the first time, a BBC observer reported on slum conditions in the East End, or unemployed working people described how they managed on the dole in 1934 they created a sensation, just as *Cathy Come Home* did in the 1960s.

But broadcasting has done a great deal more than to present the poor as victims. It has discovered the pleasures of ordinariness, creating entertainment out of nothing more than ordinary people talking about themselves, cracking jokes or doing a turn before a live audience. 'That's life' says television today, and Esther Rantzen's programme celebrates it. The first programme to do this, now long forgotten, was made in the BBC's Manchester studios for a northern working-class audience before the war. It was called *Harry Hopeful*.[16] After the war its format was borrowed by Wilfred Pickles to make *Have a Go!* – the most popular single show on radio for most of the 1950s. *Have a Go!* celebrated and affirmed the values and enjoyments of northern working-class life, but its appeal stretched far beyond Yorkshire tykes and the gradely folk of Lancashire. Equally, that most famous of television programmes, *Coronation Street*, has been enjoyed by people all over Britain ever since it began more than a quarter of a century ago.

The pleasures of broadcasting are different from other forms of entertainment and culture. Broadcasting has no sense of occasion, of a time and place set apart from day-to-day life and its affairs. The context in which people listen and watch is, in the vast majority of cases, the household.[17] And they do not listen to or watch particular programmes. They just listen or watch, with the radio or TV set on as a cheerful noise in the background, as a companionable accompaniment to other things – housework, homework, meals. In producing the world as ordinary, broadcasting has learnt over the years to adjust its services to the everyday contexts of listening and viewing, and to the ordinary lives and routines of ordinary people.[18]

From this perspective we can perhaps better understand the pleasures that are offered by *East Enders*, *Crossroads* or *Brookside*. These never-ending stories have been told, continuously for – in the case of *The Archers* – 40 years or more.[19] What makes these stories different from all others is that the characters seem to be knowable in the same way as people in the actual world are known – and this is why they appear so real to their regular devotees.

This effect is most powerfully produced by the ways in which time in the fictional world keeps pace with time in the actual world of viewers and listeners. When it's Christmas day in our world, it's Christmas in *Brookside*. Big events in the real world are taken up by the story world and occur at the same time as in reality – the most celebrated recent example being the wedding in *Coronation Street* planned to coincide with the wedding of Prince Charles and Lady Diana Spencer.

7.7. Celebrations in
Coronation Street

7.8. Ken Barlow: in first
episode of *Coronation
Street* (left) and in 1987
(right)

It is a strange experience to watch the first episode of *Coronation Street* made in grainy black and white back in 1960, and to follow it immediately with a recent episode. There, more than 25 years ago, is Ken Barlow, an anxious grammar school boy in his first year at college. And here he is now, with a chequered career and personal life behind him, an anxious middle-aged man. Such an abrupt time leap immediately makes visible the ways in which actors and characters – the two are inseparable – have aged over a quarter of a century. And this confirms the truth of the time of the tale as corresponding with the movement of lifetime and its passing away.

Since time in the fictional world and time in the actual world move together and at the same pace it follows that the lifetime of viewers and listeners unfolds at the same rate as the lives of the characters in the stories. And thus one stands in the same relation to them as one does to one's own family, friends and everyday acquaintances. What we rather disparagingly call soap operas are exemplary illustrations of the subtle and unobtrusive ways in which broadcasting runs in parallel with and interacts with the life and times of our actual world. The repetitiveness of day-to-day life, crosscut by the irreversibility of lifetime, is continuously reproduced by these stories without ending or beginning.

Today the pattern of output on radio and television is carefully adjusted to what is known of the predominant daily working, domestic and leisure routines of the whole population. Early morning radio and TV are designed to get society up and about its business for the day; the constant repetition of weather reports, traffic news, time checks and news headlines all adjust people to the mundane business of getting off to the office, factory or school on time. Programming through the day is designed for those at home; housewives, mothers, pre-school children and retired people. As households regroup in the late afternoon television news and magazine programmes resume the affairs of the day and allow people to ease into the free period of leisure and relaxation in the evening – the time when audiences for television peak.

The pleasures of the weekend are also quietly supported in ways that only become noticeable when their routine is disrupted. A few years ago the BBC shifted *Dr Who* from its traditional Saturday evening time slot, and was severely rebuked by the *Guardian* for its pains:

> All those of us who have grown up or grown old with *Dr Who*, know it to be as essential a part of a winter Saturday as coming in cold from heath, forest or football, warm crumpets (or pikelets if preferred) before the fire, the signature tune of *Sports Report*, and

that sense of liberation and escapist surrender which can only come when tomorrow is a day off too. These conditions cannot be created on Mondays and Tuesdays. Saturday will be smitten by the destruction of an essential ingredient, and *Dr Who* will be destroyed by this violent wrenching from its natural context.[20]

In these ways, broadcasting has brought together the public world and the private world, making both more accessible, supporting the routines of day-to-day life, and the changing interests and needs of people in the course of a lifetime. But the balance of power between the public and the private is not even-handed. There can be no doubt that broadcasting has opened up political, social and cultural life, and made it more democratic. But what democracy is, what it means and what it might become, is not some settled matter.[21]

Broadcasting still operates within a particular definition of democracy established back in 1918. The whole way in which radio and television deal with politics today reproduces and upholds the existing system of representative parliamentary democracy. And that in turn means that broadcasting reproduces and upholds the wider social and moral values maintained by the existing political system. Opinion *outside* this system and its values is often marginalised or denied. Many British women and many British citizens from India, Pakistan and the Caribbean argue forcefully that their interests are simply not represented in any adequate way either in British politics or in British broadcasting. Neither politics nor broadcasting as they are today can be seen as anything like the final expression of a democratic society. The continuing struggle to extend and enrich the meaning of democracy must mean extending and enriching the ways that the present system of politics and the media operate. And the pressure to do that is likely, as always, to come from outside rather than inside the institutions themselves, from the private rather than the public side of life.[22]

Further Reading

James Curran and Jean Seaton, *Power Without Responsibility. The Press and Broadcasting in Britain* (London, 1985); Robert Harris, *Gotcha! The Media, the Government and the Falklands Crisis* (London, 1983); Susan Hill, *Those Radio Times* (London, 1981); Dorothy Hobson, *Crossroads. The Drama of a Soap Opera* (London, 1982); Grace Wyndham Goldie, *Facing the Nation. Television and Politics, 1936–1976* (London, 1977); Annabelle May and Kathryn Rowan, *Inside Information: British Government and the Media* (London, 1982), a useful anthology of the ways the British state controls and manipulates the press and the broadcasters; David Morley, *Family Television: Cultural Power and Domestic Leisure* (London, 1986); Jeremy Tunstall, *The Media in Britain* (London, 1983).

People and Power

Kenneth O. Morgan

The history of labour is a vital part of the legend and the reality of modern Britain. By the end of the First World War, Britain had the most powerful and best organised working-class movement of any democratic country, perhaps of anywhere on earth. Episodes like the Tonypandy riots, the General Strike, the 1945 Labour election victory, symbols like Keir Hardie's cloth cap, are part of the folk memories of the British people. More than that, the working-class struggle, in its political form, has embodied a good deal of what the rest of the world thinks it actually means to be British. The American senator, Daniel Moynihan, once declared how important it was to understand that the leaders of the third world in Africa and Asia had received their political education from the *New Statesman*, the London School of Economics and the British Labour Party.

Yet we must focus on the *decline* as well as the *rise* of working-class politics. In fact the heyday of our labour movement was relatively brief, perhaps 20 or 30 years at best. Until the 1890s, there was no political party or organisation which represented the special interests or outlook of the workers, either in Parliament or in public life generally. The Trades Union Congress, formed in 1868, was scarcely more than a pressure-group, acting on behalf of a few, mainly craft, unions of skilled men. Only a small proportion of the workers had the vote.[1] Even after the 1884 Reform Act, the total electorate was little more than 50 per cent of the adult male population. Millions of working men still did not vote – and, of course, no women from any class had any vote at all. So far as the workers counted in politics, they were mostly staunchly Liberal. They went to chapel and worshipped God and Mr Gladstone. In some areas, notably among the textile workers of Lancashire, there were working-class Tories as well. The very idea of a separate Labour Party was a dream, perhaps even a nightmare.

Then a quite dramatic change took place in the last few years of the nineteenth century.[2] The economy was now showing the strains of foreign competition. Unemployment and a new tension in industrial relations resulted. All the evidence – from the bitter strikes of the 1880s and 1890s, to the rise of popular forms of entertainment and leisure such as the music hall and the growth of association football – suggests the presence of something new, a mature sense of working-class consciousness, class anger and class pride. Two things in particular gave all this political form.

The first was the politicisation of the *trade unions*.[3] From being rather slow-moving, inward-looking bodies, created to protect the limited interests of their members, the unions by 1914 had become powerfully enmeshed in the political process, local and national, and mobilised for action. A massive impetus in the 1890s came from the growth of the so-called 'new unionism' – the unionisation of unskilled workers in the docks, transport, gas workers, general labourers and so on. They were usually much more militant and class-conscious, as the famous London dock strike of 1889 first showed, and anxious for political involvement.

But the older unions too – the engineers, railwaymen, textile workers and the rest – slowly became aware of the need for political protection at a time of rising unemployment and trade depression, an employers' counter-attack against the unions in major strikes through the use of blackleg labour, and the hostile attitudes of the courts. These older unions were led by men who were anything but extremists. The most influential of them all was Arthur Henderson of the Iron Founders.[4] A Methodist, a teetotaller, a free trader and a staunch Liberal, he symbolised the way in which the cry for labour *independence* among the unions led on to the idea of a Labour Party. He stayed a trade union leader all his life – but he also became a Labour MP from 1903 onwards, and from 1911 secretary of the new Labour Party as well. He invented the famous phrase 'This Great Movement of Ours'. For Henderson it was almost the last of the religious crusades from which England would indeed arise and a New Jerusalem be founded.

The other vital factor was the influence of *socialism*. The very idea of it seemed alien, even unhealthy, to the majority of the workers. Karl Marx made no impact in his adopted land. Throughout the nineteenth century, socialism was linked with violence and red revolution. And yet distinct forms of British socialism began to emerge in the social and economic upheaval of the 1880s. It supplied the vital force which gave the different impulses within the trade unions the momentum to form a Labour Party. First there were the Fabian socialists, a mainly middle-class group of intellectuals based in London,[5] the most influential of them being the famous partnership of Sidney and Beatrice Webb. With their gospel of local government or 'municipal socialism', public control of the economy and a planned society, they supplied a good deal of the substance of the British idea of socialism. Then there were some Marxist socialists, too, important beyond their numbers, because of their influence amongst unskilled workers, in the 'new unions', amongst the dockers and, in due course, the miners.

Most important of all was the Independent Labour Party.[6] It was founded in 1893 at a meeting at Bradford following the growth of labour politics in the West Riding and elsewhere. It was never a mass party, yet without it working-class politics would have been very different. The ILP ensured that socialism – in the sense of the public ownership of the means of production and distribution – was always present on the labour movement's agenda. The ILP did many things. It produced famous newspapers such as the *Clarion* of Robert

8.1. Fabian meeting

8.2. Dockers, 1893

Blatchford. It campaigned in the industrial heartlands – but it also brought in notable middle-class converts. In the 1945 Labour government, men like the Prime Minister, Clement Attlee, looked back to the ILP as the channel which had brought them into the party. Above all, the ILP supplied the charismatic leaders of the pioneering years – Ramsay MacDonald, later to be Labour's first Prime Minister; Philip Snowden, later Chancellor of the Exchequer; and the inspirational cloth-cap figure of Keir Hardie, militant, pacifist, 'member for the unemployed', champion of colonial freedom. It was Hardie above all who worked out the strategy for the Alliance that the Labour Party became.[7]

The new party was founded in 1900, at the Memorial Hall, Faringdon Street, near St Paul's in London. It was a shot-gun wedding of ILP and Fabian socialists (who needed working-class support to survive) and the trade unions, who wanted a political voice after the counter-offensive of the employers and the courts in the 1890s. From the start socialists were a small minority; it was the unions who supplied the vast bulk of the membership and most of the cash. Over the next few years, indeed, one union after another affiliated to the new party. The last was the Miners' Federation in 1909 – and yet its influence over the course of working-class politics was to be the most decisive of all.[8] At first the party was simply called the Labour Representation Committee. In 1906 it was rechristened the Labour

8.3. Ramsay
MacDonald as Prime
Minister

Party and the name has stuck down to our own time.

In these very early years, the party was a loose coalition or popular front of unlikely bed-fellows. Only gradually did it build up a distinct structure and philosophy. At first it was little more than a super-pressure group to protect the workers in a hostile capitalist world. Not until 1918 did it have nationwide constituency parties. And not until then did it have its own distinctive programme when the new constitution committed Labour (through what came to be called Clause Four) to socialism. Until that time, the party was in close electoral alliance with the Liberals – indeed, it largely depended on pacts with them to survive at all. There were only 29 Labour MPs returned to Parliament in 1906, and less than 40 by the end of the First World War. Labour *did* exercise a powerful influence on the Liberal and Conservative parties, of course. The social reforms of the Liberal Chancellor of the Exchequer, Lloyd George, down to 1914 were in some measure the result of fear of labour and of class conflict.[9] But the Labour Party, as a small third force on the fringes of power, could do little enough on its own.

The First World War, though, brought immense changes. Liberalism died in the trenches. The Liberals were fatally divided between followers of Asquith and of Lloyd George; they were also losing support in industrial regions and Labour reaped the benefit. Again, the war had led to a huge extension of democracy which also helped Labour. In the 1918 Reform Act, the vote was extended to virtually all adult males and to all women over 30 as well. The electorate went up from 8 million to 21 million. Industrial districts like the coalfields of South Wales, Yorkshire and the North East, inner-city areas like the East End of London or the centre of Glasgow became impregnable working-class strongholds. The war brought something else as well. This was the heady impact of the Russian Revolution.[10] The stirring events in Russia, the fall of the hated Czarist empire, the dawn of a new kind of workers' and peasants' republic in the Soviet Union, had something of the impact for British workers and radicals that the revolution in France had had in 1789. Lenin even thought Britain itself might be the next country caught up in popular insurrection – though he was proved wrong. The outcome was that Labour clearly emerged as the democratic voice of the British left, and actually formed the government in 1924.

In the inter-war years, the two decisive episodes were the 1926 General Strike and the 1931 political crisis which set up the so-called National government. Both had a huge impact on working-class attitudes. The General Strike exploded for ever the myth of workers' direct action, mobilised to bring down the elected government of the day. What happened in 1931 was a huge defeat, but one from which the party emerged clearer in its ideas and stronger in the constituencies.

The 1926 General Strike came at a time of heavy unemployment, especially in the coalfields.[11] It arose from the confrontation of the

8.4. The end of the General Strike

private coalowners, intent on massive wage cuts, and the militant Miners' Federation. Reluctantly, the TUC were dragged in. For nine days in May 1926, millions of workers throughout the country were out on strike. The class war seemed terrifyingly close at hand. But the TUC always wanted a settlement and soon pulled out. Later in the year, the miners, who had fought on alone, had to capitulate to the coalowners and the Tory government, broken and dispirited. Most trade unionists now forgot about dreams of industrial action, and swung with new zest to support the Labour Party. A dream had faded: 1926 would never be forgotten in communities like the mining villages of South Wales or Durham – but neither would it be repeated.

The events of 1931 arose from a massive run on the pound.[12] The second Labour government split in two over proposed cuts in unemployment benefit, and its prime minister, Ramsay MacDonald, defected to lead a National government, including the Conservatives and most of the Liberals as well. The 1931 crisis in some ways saw the Labour Party at its worst. It was quite unable to cope with a collapse in the industrial and financial system. Indeed, it scarcely had any sensible economic policy at all. Yet on the other hand, the decision of the party and the TUC, led by the veteran Arthur Henderson, to oppose the National government was in the long run a blessing. The Labour Party suffered huge losses in the 1931 general election. But it emerged potentially stronger from the experience. The party still kept its broad trade union base to help it recover from the trauma of 1931. It rebuilt its strength in its old industrial strongholds. It pushed into new urban areas such as Liverpool, Birmingham and Cardiff where it had hitherto been comparatively weak. And in addition Labour could now develop much clearer ideas and policies. Under the centrist leadership of men such as Attlee, Herbert Morrison and Hugh Dalton, it sorted out its difficulties over foreign policy and rearmament. In its home policy, it evolved a kind of mixture of democratic socialism and Keynesian-style planning. By the Second World War – really for the first time in its history – Labour looked like a party fit to govern and to wield power.[13]

These crucial years of the Labour movement, however, were much more than a routine exercise in parliamentary politics. They meant, above all, a transformation in *local* communities and their structures of power. In the 1920s and 1930s, Labour gradually won control of more and more local authorities. In 1934 the great prize of the London County Council, led by Herbert Morrison, fell to the party.[14] Labour councils were in the front line in protecting working men and women against the effects of mass unemployment, in resisting the impact of the means test for social insurance, in defending standards in education, housing and the social services. For most people, it was

Labour leadership at the local, familiar level that expressed the reality of democratic socialism, British-style.

There was also a special dimension in Scotland and Wales.[15] Labour grew up by condemning the semi-nationalism of the Celtic fringe, the 'little Bethel stage of Wales for the Welsh', to quote one ILP newspaper. It upheld the cause of workers in all countries, irrespective of nation, creed or language. Yet there was always a distinctive Scottish and Welsh aspect of the party as it grew up. There was even a Welsh-language Labour newspaper, *Llais Llafur*, the Voice of Labour. The Scottish aspect was very pronounced among the militant MPs from Clydeside in the 1920s. Interestingly, most of them, men like Jimmy Maxton, were Scottish home rulers as well as left-wing socialists and advocates of the 'living wage'. In Wales, Labour made huge inroads in the mining valleys of South Wales in the inter-war years. One young miners' MP, Aneurin Bevan of Ebbw Vale, poured scorn on the very idea of Celtic separatism. How did Welsh sheep differ from English sheep? he asked ironically. And yet, in spite of himself, Bevan and the Welsh Labour movement were also the heirs of the old Liberalism of the chapels and the *eisteddfod*, of working-class education, and the close ties of community life. In fact, the Labour movement was to prove immensely strong in Scotland and Wales from the 1920s down to the 1970s. It was not just because of the heavy industries and mass unemployment there, but also because Labour, as an undogmatic popular coalition, could reflect the common culture and history of the Welsh and Scottish people.

From 1945, Labour emerged from being a party of protest into a party of power. It was no longer on the outside looking in. The Second World War itself helped greatly in this process.[16] There was a sense of national solidarity and of common sacrifice in the blitz and on the battlefield. Labour ministers such as Attlee and Ernest Bevin were prominent in Churchill's coalition – 1945 was their victory, too. And the war also brought great radical blueprints like the Beveridge Plan for social security, with which Labour was closely identified in sympathy. But the huge Labour victory of 1945, when 393 Labour MPs were returned and Clement Attlee became Prime Minister, was also rooted in more profound changes – in those intellectual and social shifts in the 1930s which saw new visions of collective action and social and economic planning. Labour not only captured power in 1945. It was also, for the first time in its history, ready to use it.

The Attlee government of 1945–51 provided a rare moment of unity and achievement.[17] It has been ever since the basic point of reference for all Labour politicians. It created much of the fabric of the welfare state, notably Aneurin Bevan's National Health Service and the National Insurance scheme of another Welshman, James

8.5. The 'Clydeside Reds'

8.6. The Labour Victory of 1945

Griffiths. More controversially, it passed eight major measures of public ownership, and took nearly a quarter of the economy into state hands. Above all, it maintained full employment. It removed the terrible scourge of depression and industrial decline from Scotland, Wales and the North of England. Overseas, it achieved the transfer of power in India and Pakistan, and the launch of the new Commonwealth. The fact, too, that Britain was one of the 'big three' at the end of the war gave its Foreign Secretary, Ernest Bevin, great prestige. It meant that Labour could play the patriotic card. To a socialist minister like Nye Bevan, Britain stood for the democratic socialist 'middle way', neither capitalist nor communist, a beacon of hope to the shattered and demoralised world.

What we notice about this Attlee government is that, uniquely among Labour administrations, it had a powerful sense of internal *unity*. This was because Attlee's Cabinet led from the top. It was widely respected and generally obeyed. The parliamentary party, Transport House, the National Executive and the annual party conference were, for once in a while, solidly lined up in support of the government. Most important of all, the labour alliance was firmly endorsed by the TUC and by the leaders of major unions like the miners and the transport workers. The ordinary workers seemed to feel that this was *their* government, maintaining fair shares and full employment, creating the welfare state, building houses and new schools.

The key figures in the Attlee government were the wily political manager, Herbert Morrison, who orchestrated the party at all levels, and the massive figure of Ernie Bevin of the Transport Workers, the physical embodiment of the solidarity of labour and the loyal support of the unions. Morrison and Bevin hated each other – and yet they formed an essential partnership. As a result of their activities, morale was generally high in the party in these difficult post-war years. The unions could put up with austerity, rationing and limited expectations all round. Party membership was high and rising. When the Attlee government was finally defeated in October 1951, it polled more votes than did the victorious Conservatives, more even than it had polled in the historic year of 1945.

Yet the end of the Attlee government also heralded a phase of internal, long-term decline. This arose from deep within the heart of the movement. Trade unions came to resent the government's controls on wage bargaining and union freedom. The mighty figure of Aneurin Bevan, who resigned from the Attlee government in April 1951 when a huge rearmament programme led to charges being imposed on his National Health Service, provided a focus for fierce internal argument over both foreign and domestic policy, which raged for years to come.[18] The period of Conservative government, between 1951 and 1964, was a time of constant Labour internal rows. Many of them were concerned with foreign policy, with German rearmament as a part of western defence, with the alliance with the United States, most traumatically with nuclear disarmament and Britain's possession of the atomic and hydrogen bombs. But more fundamentally, the very idea of socialism, whether the Attlee government could really be said to have built up in any sense a socialist Britain, created fierce divisions within the party, with the supporters of the left-winger Nye Bevan, and the right-winger, the former Chancellor of the Exchequer, Hugh Gaitskell, warring furiously against each other. In 1959 there was even an attempt to remove the socialist commitment to nationalisation of the means of production and of distribution from the party programme and constitution. It is significant that it failed, due to deep opposition from major trade unions as well as from socialists in the constituency parties. But it is even more significant that the question should be raised at all. The debate over Clause Four and nationalisation suggested a deep uncertainty and doubt at the very heart of British socialism, whether the creed of class warfare and fundamental economic transformation really applied any more to an increasingly homogeneous and affluent society such as mid-twentieth-century Britain.

Then in 1964 there came the fresh figure of Harold Wilson to provide, it seemed, a new focus of unity.[19] Wilson had a left-wing past, though he used right-wing rhetoric and ideas. He argued that socialism was concerned not with class war, but with science, industrial modernisation and economic growth. He won the 1964 election, narrowly, on this programme and then retained power in 1966 with a majority of nearly a hundred. Some believed that Attlee's old ambition to make Labour the natural majority party, based on the unions but also winning the support of the socially-concerned middle class and of intellectuals generally, might now be in sight. But it all proved to be an illusion. A government, supposedly consisting of planners and experts, crucially failed to plan. The economy was frequently almost out of control, unemployment began to rise, the pound was devalued. Labour in office seemed incompetent. There was a decline in morale and membership in the constituencies in marked contrast to the enthusiasm of the years after 1945. Worst of all, the alliance of the political and industrial wings of the movement, so central to the party ever since its foundation, began to split asunder. The unions' rejection of any idea of an incomes policy or wage restraint led to a huge crisis which gravely weakened the stature of the government. The unity and fraternalism of the 1945 period markedly disintegrated. Labour fell from office in 1970 with its lowest share of the poll since the 1930s. Since then there has been no sustained recovery.

If the years down to 1945, perhaps even down to 1966, have in some respects seen the emergence and maturity of working-class politics in Britain, the period since the election of the Wilson government has, equally clearly, seen their decline.[20] A number of deep-rooted forces, latent in the party since the 1950s, have become ever more apparent. Labour has found difficulty in retaining its working-class constituency; it has been internally divided; while the idea of socialism is less able to offer acceptable and credible guidelines.

The first factor that has become very plain is the break-up of the historic working class, the very bedrock of the organised labour movement. Even in Scotland and Wales, these forces of disintegration have been going on apace. The old staple industries, built on coalpits, steelworkers and shipyards, have been eroding steadily since the 1950s. The Labour Party's great strength always lay in one-industry, homogeneous, working-class communities, perhaps even in industrial villages. In the 1930s, it was as strong in the pit villages of South Wales or the textile towns of the West Riding as it was relatively weak in Greater London. Since the 1950s, these communities have become denuded, and most of their old community life has disappeared with them. When new industries were brought into Wales, Scotland and the North in the 1950s and 1960s, they subtly changed the nature of

8.7. Welsh coalminers during the 1950s

8.8. Clement Attlee
visits the Cup Final as
Prime Minister, 1948

Labour's heartland. The workers were often commuters, their home
bases becoming ghost towns during the day. The Labour Party, it has
been said, has been as much a part of the historic working class as was
the growth of professional football. Both saw their heyday after 1945;
both declined together thereafter. Perhaps it is symbolic that the one
great popular landmark of Harold Wilson's premiership in the 1960s
was that England won the World Cup in 1966.

The decline of the old working class has also seen the declining
political influence of the trade unions. Union membership has slumped
during the economic difficulties of the 1970s and 1980s. The close
relationship between the unions and the Labour Party, inherent in the
founding of the party and built into the structure of the 1918
constitution which underlined the unions' dominance at all levels, is
now weakened. A growing number of unions, of course, are white-
collar in membership. Even in 1945, there was a close identification
between the TUC and the Attlee government. The contrast between
that mood of partnership and the open conflict of 1969 when the
unions turned on their own party, and even more the 'winter of
discontent' in 1978–9 when union disaffection largely brought down
the last Labour government, is stark indeed. The unions are now a
beleaguered pressure group, concerned largely with self-defence on a
narrow front, rather than with winning and mobilising power right
across society.

The remaining working class, too, is apparently less radical. Partly this may be because of Labour's own record of success after 1945 – and also the way in which post-war Conservative governments down to 1974 followed much of the Attlee government's programme. With most workers secure in their jobs, owning their own homes, with rising expectations in terms of household possessions and holiday travel, the traditional message of a Labour Party, conceived in the back-to-back loyalties of working-class terraces, too often seems drab and lacking in inspiration. Large numbers of working-class people still live in squalid surroundings, especially in decaying industrial areas in the North. But the bulk of their fellow citizens do not, and feel a diminished sense of solidarity with those less fortunate.

The very idea of socialism, too, is much less compelling than it used to be. Keir Hardie and the early prophets of the ILP made their evangelistic form of socialism the centrepiece of their creed. To a lesser extent, this was even true of the government of 1945 as well. Labour activists in the 1960s and 1970s, in the constituency parties especially, still proclaimed neo-Marxist certainties about class division and the coming collapse of capitalism. But this has been less and less attractive to the electorate in general. One interesting litmus test is the declining appeal of nationalisation.[21] In 1945, it was in the forefront of Labour's message and its election programme, 'Let us Face the Future'. It meant that the mines, the railways, steelworks and much else besides would truly belong to the people. Yet, in fact, doubts about nationalisation arose even then. In 1951, Labour went to the country with no specific nationalisation proposals in its manifesto at all. The party has made less and less of this specifically socialist panacea ever since.

The decline of socialism has gone along with something else, something especially apparent in the past 20 years. This is the declining legitimacy and moral authority of the *state*. Labour's programme was always linked with a major role for central government. The gentleman in Whitehall knew best. Partly through dislike of bureaucracy, partly because of a flagging faith in all our public institutions among a more disenchanted world, state action no longer looks like the answer to all our woes. To the Fabians in the 1920s, the planners of the 1930s, to Cripps in the 1940s, it seemed too obvious that state intervention would eliminate injustices, redistribute wealth, above all, provide a creed of public service, in place of the selfish ethic of private capitalism under which the weakest went to the wall. But by the end of the 1970s, all this seemed more and more unpalatable. It was a god that had failed. This meant that not only the ideas of working-class politics were disintegrating. Their instruments of action were doing so as well.

It is much too early to pronounce a requiem for British working-class politics. In so many ways, it has invigorated and humanised modern Britain. Partly through the direct work of the Labour Party, nationally and locally, partly through the impact on other parties, Labour has made life far more bearable for the great mass of citizens. Socialist intellectuals such as the Webbs, Laski, Tawney, Cole and Crosland have enriched our cultural life and been a powerhouse of ideas. Middle-class politicians from Attlee downwards have been brought in through a sense of social service, while generations of working-class leaders have found new public outlets for their abilities. The very existence of the British labour movement is a major reason why Britain did not see the kind of large Communist Party that sprang up in Italy or France. Yet the sense of decline is inescapable.

What remains of this movement today? Curiously enough, there is a strong sense of history. Labour, more than perhaps any other political movement in our country, celebrates the past – its own alternative past. Not a history of battles, of royal pomp and circumstance, but the saga of Tonypandy, the General Strike and the Jarrow march, and the values enshrined in the 1945 Attlee government. The heroes and heroines of Labour's past provide coherence, unity, inspiration. So we are left with a paradox. A party that worships the collective ideal gets its stimulus from the cult of personality. A movement created to establish a future socialist commonwealth finds constant renewal through an appeal to the ages.

Further Reading

Eric Hobsbawm, *Labouring Men* (London, 1964, paperback edn, 1986); Henry Pelling, *The Origins of the Labour Party, 1880–1900* (London, 1954: currently in Oxford paperback); E.H. Phelps Brown, *The Origins of Trade Union Power* (Oxford, 1983: currently in Oxford paperback); Ben Pimlott, *Labour and the Left in the 1930s* (Cambridge, 1977: London paperback edn, 1986); Kenneth O. Morgan, *Labour in Power, 1945–1951* (Oxford, 1984: currently in Oxford paperback); Kenneth O. Morgan, *Labour People. Leaders and Lieutenants, Hardie to Kinnock* (Oxford, 1987).

CHAPTER NINE

The Myth of Consensus

Ben Pimlott

Politics contains fashionable words and phrases that are soon on everybody's lips, acquiring the status of instant explanation. Some quickly vanish: others linger, become universally absorbed, and gain a permanent niche in our vocabulary — shaping and perhaps distorting the way in which we view our world.

Consensus is one such word. It is a long-established term, but one which has gained an important place in British political parlance only during the last decade. Especially since Mrs Thatcher took office in 1979 and began to introduce major changes, the view has gained wide acceptance that British politics used to be characterised by a consensus, but that this nation-uniting mood no longer exists.

The alleged consensus has been regarded in different ways. For some, particularly on the political right, it was disastrously misconceived: an ostrich-like refusal to accept hard economic facts, a wrongheaded conventional wisdom that led to the crises of the 1970s. For others, especially in the centre and centre-left of the political spectrum, the supposed consensus was the cause of much that has been good, a fertile source of progressive social and economic policy, and the basis for a more harmonious and less divided society. Whether the consensus has been villain or hero — whether its passing is celebrated or mourned — few of the writers, journalists and politicians who need to give contemporary politics a reference point doubt that it once existed.

The proper instinct of any critical observer of affairs, when confronted with near unanimity, is to query its assumptions. I want to consider the assumptions behind this notion of a consensus and look at the way in which the proposition that it once existed but does so no more has shaped our perceptions of political events in the twentieth century.

Consensus is Latin for agreement, and like many Latin terms, its first use in English was scientific. Physiologists spoke of a *consensus* to describe an agreement or harmony of organs of the body which had a specific purpose. In the middle of the last century, the term began to be used to refer to the body politic, but with the anatomical usage still in mind.

In the twentieth century the physiological origin has been forgotten, and the link consciously discarded. Nevertheless, the organic metaphor remains embedded in our modern understanding of the term. Consensus in political language is certainly a more powerful and emotive term than mere agreement. Consensus is said to exist not when people merely agree, but when they are happy agreeing, are not constrained to agree, and leave few of their number outside the broad parameters of their agreement. Thus in the modern – as in the old-fashioned – sense of the term, a consensus is a harmony. Further, those who are a part of it frequently share a purpose, in a way that is analogous to the common purpose of bodily organs.

Consensus generally carries with it a value element. The idea of a consensus is a positive thing – better again than mere acceptance or agreement. People seek to 'embrace', 'capture' and 'influence' the consensus, and are proud to claim possession of it. In politics, it is often seen in national terms. The philosopher Comte thought of it as something which held society together, with much more at stake than a single issue. It was to him a habit of mind from which disagreement was largely absent. Consensus is not based on a head count and has no formal expression. This in itself makes the very concept of consensus hard to pin down. Yet it does imply freedom of choice. It would be odd to talk of consensus under a Hitler or a Stalin. Normally consensus is regarded as the product of the free flow of ideas in a liberal society where the shared attitudes of men and women may have some influence over events. Consensus is to a free country what fear is to an unfree one.

Harmony, purpose, freedom. There is no rigid definition, but there is certainly both a history and an appropriate context. The question now arises: can we pinpoint a particular, historic British consensus, cast in such terms, that goes beyond shared values about constitutional rules, and represents a temporary yet substantial unity of opinion on how major policy should proceed?

Those who have outlined such a consensus have presented a tale of narrative simplicity, with a beginning, a middle and an end. It runs as follows, and we should consider its contours closely.

The origins of this consensus, according to the accepted version, are to be found in an earlier period of disunity and political strife, when agreement existed only on some basic national arrangements, such as the rule of law and the sovereignty of Crown and Parliament. Even on these, there had frequently been bitter disagreement. Thus, up to 1914 fierce and irreconcilable divisions – over the status of Ireland, the rights of trade unions, free trade, the extension of the suffrage – had threatened social stability. The First World War, so far from healing rifts, exacerbated them, and in the 1920s conflict over Ireland reached its bloody climax, while an angry labour movement challenged the power of the state. Even when a 'National' coalition was formed in 1931, it was National in little more than name, serving mainly to emphasise the depth of division. In the 1930s, political opinion was fiercely split on all major issues, and Britain remained a divided and antagonistic society, kept apart by differences of wealth, class, education, occupation and region.

Nevertheless – according to the argument I am describing – it is precisely in this period that the seeds of later agreement are to be found. The very clash of ideas provided fertile ground for conciliatory proposals aimed at bridging the gap between opposed social forces. Such, in particular, was the purpose of the *General Theory* of Maynard Keynes, which advocated an expansionist solution to the rigours of the slump. Such, too, was the objective of parallel suggestions, receiving cross-party support, for measures of state planning.

From these beginnings, so it is maintained, a mighty oak soon grew.

9.1. Lady Astor

9.2. Poster encouraging electors to vote for the National Government 1931

The official birthday of the 'post-war consensus' – according to true believers – was May 1940, when Winston Churchill took office at the head of a genuine coalition (in contrast to that of 1931), the most broad-based government this country has ever known. Paul Addison, author of a classic book about wartime domestic policy, *The Road to 1945*, and a leading evangelist of the consensus thesis, writes that:

> in the course of time, the Coalition proved to be the greatest reforming administration since the Liberal government of 1905–14.[1]

Great emphasis is placed on the war years by the consensus theorists – both enthusiasts like Addison, and critics such as Corelli Barnett[2] – because it is on this key period of emergency-created cooperation that their whole case rests. And there is no doubt that this *was* a remarkably innovative episode, in which politicians of all parties – as well as permanent and temporary civil servants – played a part.

The need to streamline the economy to meet the requirements of total war, the need to maintain civilian morale and give people something to work for, the red-tape-cutting dynamism which Churchill's own personality engendered: all these led to a string of reforms, on which there was undoubtedly wide agreement. Thus, during the period 1940–3, universal social security, family allowances, a root-and-branch educational reform, the main features of a national health service, a revolutionary new approach to budgetary policy, had all been placed on the agenda. At the same time, the policy goal of full employment, together with ideas about town and country planning and government intervention in industry, was gaining acceptance.

It is here, according to its proponents, that the British consensus theory takes off. Four events, practical and symbolic, are presented as foundation stones. The first – arguably the most important – was the pioneering 'Keynesian' budget of Sir Kingsley Wood in 1941, the result of Maynard Keynes's direct influence in the Treasury, as economic adviser. The second was the famous Beveridge Report on Social Insurance and Allied Services in 1942 – blueprint for the post-war welfare state. The other two both occurred in 1944, and were directed towards a post-war world already in sight. One was R.A.

9.3. Unemployed men in Manchester, 1938

9.4. Mill girls during their lunch break

Butler's Education Act which raised the school-leaving age and provided free secondary education for all children, including grammar school places for a lucky minority; the other was an Employment Policy White Paper, whose full-employment goal was accepted by all three political parties.

On each of these measures, reports and statements there was some disagreement but on none, point out the 'consensus' historians, was disagreement fundamental. 'All three parties went to the polls in 1945 committed to principles of social and economic reconstruction' writes Addison; '. . . the new consensus of the war years', he sums up, 'was positive and purposeful'.[3]

And so, according to the consensus argument, it remained. A Labour government, elected in July 1945 with Clement Attlee as Prime Minister, inherited the 'positive and purposeful' wartime consensus and proceed to carry out many of the reforms which had been developed in principle during the Coalition years, some of which were already in the administrative pipeline. Eventually defeated in the election of 1951, Labour passed on the mantle to a new look Tory

Party, which quietly endorsed and even embraced them. Meanwhile, economic reconstruction and the Cold War forced both major parties to tie Britain's fate closely to that of the United States, bringing Labour and Tory foreign policies into agreement.

Here, then, we have the widely proclaimed British consensus — alternatively billed as a golden age of rising living standards, domestic and European peace, full employment and social improvement; or as locust years of spendthrift state socialism leading to national decline. The high priest of this era is often presented as Harold Macmillan, Vicky's 'Supermac', who combined in his chameleon personality old and new, ancient and modern, right and left. A crofter's grandson who married a duke's daughter, his manners were those of a grandee, but his background belonged to the progressive publishing world of Bloomsbury: Maynard Keynes had been a childhood friend, and Macmillan's pre-war book, *The Middle Way*,[4] scriptural text for the consensus-minded, helped to inject Keynesian thought into British politics.

Macmillan resigned in 1963, but — so it is generally maintained — the consensus which he led and epitomised survived him. There are different opinions about when it is supposed finally to have come to an end. Some believe that a deepening divide was already visible by the time of the 1970 election, when Edward Heath's 'Selsdon Man' proposals seemed to mark a Conservative shift to the right. For others, the turning-point was the 1973–4 miners' strike. The most decisive moment, however, is frequently seen as the 1979 election, after which Mrs Thatcher inaugurated a new kind of radical Conservatism, consciously distancing herself, not only from Labour policy, but also from past Tory practice. This allegedly consensus-breaking tilt by the government was soon to be paralleled by Labour's tilt to the left, leading to the fissure that saw the launching of the SDP, and an enlarged centre-grouping between the now distant major party blocks.

Like most historical theories, the consensus thesis is as much about the present as the past. The assumption of harmony in the past is a way of underlining the gulf that is believed to exist in the present. Thus, it is often argued that the 'end of consensus' has altered the parameters of debate. The 'consensus' theory is invoked in order to argue that a much broader spectrum of opinion now exists, characterised at the extremes by an authoritarian, anti-bureaucratic, privatising and nationalistic Conservatism, and by a directive, union-orientated, neutralist socialism.

Looking back over the past 50 years, this theory of the British consensus certainly provides a neat, convenient explanatory frame-work, containing as it does a period of general prosperity and accelerating expectations which had a very different tone from our own. Few would dispute that 1940 marked the start of something new; while the sense of a sea-change in British politics during the 1970s has certainly been widely felt.

Yet the notion that major changes have occurred in prevailing ideas, even if demonstrably true, does not necessarily entail a lost consensus. We need to consider the possibility, indeed, that the consensus is a mirage, an illusion that rapidly fades the closer one gets to it. We may argue, against the popular theory of the consensus, that genuine consensus in politics is very rare and, further, that we see more agreement in the past than in the present. The heat and passion of current controversy always seems to burn more fiercely while it is actually happening, than later, when tempers have cooled. In retrospect, the cause of a past dispute may often seem a trifle, and the historian may be struck by the closeness of rival points of view.

It is possible that both the nostalgic and the rejectionist historians have fallen into this trap, committing the grievous error of anachronism. For – taking the period of supposed 'consensus' from the Second World War to Mrs Thatcher – there is little sign of the main political actors regarding themselves as part of a 'national consensus' at the time.

True, politicians of all parties, as well as civil servants and academic writers, were profoundly influenced by the giant figures of William Beveridge and Maynard Keynes. It is also true that the right in British politics is less deferential towards the ideas of these thinkers than was true of many leading Conservatives 20 or 30 years ago. But this scarcely proves the previous existence of a 'consensus'.

One reason for increased criticism of Beveridge and Keynes is simply that they spoke to a different age: their remedies were offered as solutions to problems that no longer present themselves in the same way. Such criticism comes, of course, from left as well as right, as people of all kinds try to come to terms with a world in which old principles – for example those which used to provide full employment – no longer seem to operate. As modern practitioners and thinkers distance themselves from earlier approaches, there is a tendency to think in terms of a past unity. Yet this is incorrect.

Neither Beveridge, nor Keynes, nor any of the other leading theorists and policy-makers of their time offered anything that could be regarded as a gospel. There was never a body of literature that constituted a sacred text, never an orthodoxy towards which dutiful political leaders or officials could guide the ship of state. Neither Beveridge nor Keynes was a Marx or a Lenin, and their suggestions were only gradually accepted, and never in their entirety.

The old Treasury, wedded to classical economics and the 'saving candle-ends' philosophy of William Gladstone, fought a staunch rearguard action against the radical monetary and fiscal plans of Keynes, who continued to arouse deep suspicion, both on the left of the Labour Party, which rightly saw Keynesianism as an alternative to socialism, and among the Tory right. 'Butskellism' was the sardonic term coined to describe the alleged continuity between the economic policies of Labour's Hugh Gaitskell and his Tory successor at the Treasury, R.A. Butler. The use of the word, however, certainly did not indicate a consensus. Rather, it was a term of abuse, a sign of a widespread disapproval which was harmful to the reputations of both men.

Like Keynes, Beveridge was a Liberal whose ideas married well with Fabian socialist thought. Not every socialist supported Beveridge: one fierce critic of the 1942 Beveridge Report was Ernest Bevin, the trade union leader and wartime Minister of Labour; nevertheless, the 1945 Labour government took up the Report as its own, and implemented or adapted many of its proposals, which embodied the principle of universality in the provision of state benefits. Conservatives subsequently accepted what Labour had done, and no government (not even the present one) has ever ventured to advocate the abolition of the welfare state. Yet the notion that Tory paternalists had as much to do with extending the social role of the state as Labour welfarists, is folklore of the kind disseminated by Conservative Central Office at election time, or by Marxists keen to discredit the 'bourgeois' Labour Party. Few political battles have been as bitter as Nye Bevan's fight with the Tory-backed doctors over the creation of the Health Service. Few ideological strands have been as consistent as the Tories' hostility towards treating the 'undeserving poor' – latterly renamed 'welfare scroungers' – with generosity. Conservative opposition to the principles of universality, always latent, became increasingly vocal from the mid 1960s – almost a quarter of a century before Mrs Thatcher came to power.[5]

It is easy to take for granted hard-won reforms, and to forget how bitterly they were contested at the time. When one policy triumphs over another, it is tempting to regard the change as inevitable, and as part of a progressive, consensual evolution. Yet the reality of radical reform is that it has seldom come without a fight.

Take, for instance, the wartime Coalition, that great reforming administration whose spirit of cooperation supposedly gave rise to the post-war consensus. We need not dispute the importance for domestic policy of the initiatives of the 1940–5 period in order to observe that the public amity of Churchill's government masked deep ideological conflicts. Few proposals, indeed, were the subject of more bitter inter-party disputes than those of Sir William Beveridge, regarded by some

9.5. Winston Churchill, 1951

Tory leaders as a perilous hostage to fortune, and by most of the Labour Party as a banner to fight under. For a time, there was a serious possibility that the Coalition might break up.

Tensions that had existed between wartime ministerial partners, yet had been hushed up because of the political truce, surfaced as soon as Labour left the government following the defeat of Hitler. No election has been fought more ferociously, or with more immoderate language, than that of 1945 – in which Churchill accused Labour of plotting to set up a 'gestapo', as serious an allegation, within weeks of the opening of the death camps, as it is possible to imagine.

'Thank God for the civil service', King George VI is supposed to have said, when the result of the poll was known. Labour's assumption of power was marked by continuity, not by upheaval, and this has encouraged a later belief that the important measures which followed were the product of a 'consensus' rather than of socialism. A reading of the press at the time will swiftly banish such a notion. Tory Opposition in Parliament was initially weak, partly because of the surprising scale of Labour's victory. Yet Labour's programme was fiercely resisted and furiously resented. The progressive and egalitarian taxation policies and low interest rate policy of the Labour Chancellor, for example, particularly outraged the City of London.

Take, too, the allegedly Butskellite 1950s, when Conservative chancellors continued some of the policies established by their Labour predecessors. Here there was agreement of a kind between the two front benches and the Treasury, though scarcely amounting to a 'consensus'. Huge differences between the parties remained. There was certainly no element of me-tooism about Anthony Crosland's impassioned plea for greater social equality, *The Future of Socialism*, which was published in 1956 and conceived, not as a statement for the middle-of-the-road and the consensus-minded, but as a radical alternative to prevailing Tory attitudes.

What about followers, as distinct from leaders? Did they at least share a 'consensus'? The American scholar, Samuel Beer, in his book *Britain Against Itself*, argues that consensus existed in the 1950s and 1960s because 'party government had given rise to an agreement on the common good which, to be sure, fell far short of unanimity, but which did accomplish the aggregation of the preferences of a large majority of the electorate'.[6] Yet even this is far from clear. Indeed we may go further. Whatever lines of continuity or discontinuity may have existed at the top, ordinary voters appear to have been *more* divided during the period of the so-called consensus than since its supposed conclusion.

In an age of agreement, even of agreement that fell short of unanimity, it would be reasonable to expect the electorate to care little which party held office. Consensus-mindedness might also seem conducive to the growth of a centre party, which could best express the shared values, and lack of partnership, of much of the nation. In fact, throughout the key years of the supposed consensus, rigid loyalty to one major party or the other was the norm, and switching the exception, while the political centre was at its most insignificant. True, there was electoral tranquillity of sorts. Opinion shifted little from one general election to the next. From 1950 to 1970 the Conservative vote was never outside the range 43.5–49.5 per cent, or the Labour vote outside 43–49. This tranquillity – in contrast to the volatility of before the war, or of the last decade and a half – has been offered as evidence of consensus. A moment's thought will show it as the reverse. Sandbagged in their electoral trenches, the early post-war voters can be seen as the anonymous infantry of two implacably opposed armies in an era of adversarial politics, with the middle-way Liberals floundering in no-man's-land.

It may of course be argued that the electoral preferences of citizens reflect culture and class rather than discriminating policy choices and hence the refusal of voters to vary their allegiances is quite compatible with a basic agreement, across party lines, on the issues of the day. This is a difficult case to sustain, however. On the one hand, it is surely contradictory to claim voters for the consensus, while discounting their behaviour at the ballot box. On the other hand, social and cultural loyalties (identification with a class, in particular) were just as important before the Second World War, when voters were much more fickle in their loyalties, as after it.

But the greatest problem for the consensus theory is in defining the essence of the consensus itself, that ghostly cloak which, we are assured, encompassed our national life through happy or wastrel years. I began by discussing the origins and usage of the term consensus, and then examined the topography of the supposed British one. Yet what, even notionally, does the terrain amount to? The British post-war consensus could be defined, not entirely flippantly, as the product of a consensus among historians about those political ideas that should be regarded as important, and hence to be used as touchstones of the consensus. Neither is it irrelevant to consider the political orientation of those historians from whom the consensus thesis is derived. Some – the rejectionists – bolster their sympathy for modern Conservatism by contrasting it with the alleged compromises of the past. Others, probably the majority, display towards the kind of policy package they choose to label 'consensus' a shamelessly sentimental yearning.

According to both groups of writers, we now live in a post-consensus age, in which a 'monetarist' Conservative Party is confronted by the 'collectivist' forces of Labour. Many instances of division, indeed, are cited to illustrate the recent 'breakdown of consensus'. Yet we may wonder whether in future, when the dust has settled, division will appear so much sharper than before. To take the most obvious comparison: if it was a Tory Chancellor, Kingsley Wood, who opened the first Keynesian budget in 1941, it was a Labour Chancellor, Denis Healey, who was responsible for the first monetarist budget in 1976, three years before Mrs Thatcher took office. The monetarist/collectivist distinction possibly made some sense at the beginning of the 1980s, after Labour's lurch to the left. With contemporary Labour leaders seeking to outdo each other in their eagerness to abandon public ownership and to minimise central economic direction, the distinction can scarcely be given much credence today. It would, indeed, be surprising if all of the new principles and practices established at the Treasury in the years of Howe and Lawson were to be abandoned when a non-Conservative administration eventually comes to power.

What will the consensus-hunters of the future find to say about the late 1980s? Much more, I would wager, than it is yet easy to perceive. Distance makes it possible to look beyond the emotion and the invective, and see prevailing attitudes which, because shared and uncontentious, do not hit the headlines and may not even be noticed at the time. But this is not to say that the visible differences – some of which are harsh and desperate – are not real.

The same may be true of the period after the Second World War. Then, as now, events were as much determined by dispute as by cooperation. 'Consensus' is a handy piece of jargon, with a pleasant resonance, to describe a time when we were all younger, more eager or more foolish. But whether it will survive as a term for a discrete episode in British history — instead of joining other phrases in the dustbin of historiography — is to be doubted.

Further Reading

R. Barker, *Political Ideas in Modern Britain* (London, 1978); C. Barnett, *The Audit of War* (London, 1987); S.H. Beer, *Modern British Politics: A Study of Parties and Pressure Groups* (London, 1965); W. Keegan, *Mrs Thatcher's Economic Experiment* (London, 1984); A. Marwick, *Britain in the Century of Total War* (London, 1968); K. Middlemass, *Politics in Industrial Society: The Experience of the British System since 1911* (London, 1979); Kenneth O. Morgan, *Labour in Power 1945–51* (Oxford, 1985); A. Seldon (ed.), *The Emerging Consensus* (London, 1981).

CHAPTER TEN

The Dark Strangers

Michael Gilkes

Immigrants! Today the word is loaded with our cumulative fears and prejudices, conjuring up a picture of dark aliens and refugees; the detritus of other, less developed or less fortunate nations who might pose a threat to our own stable society and culture. But the word is not only emotive, it is also double-edged. Immigrants are, in a sense, always exiles, emigrants forced by circumstances to leave their own homes for the adventure of life in another country.

Behind every arrivant lies the trauma of departure. Immigrants do not arrive as blank figures or statistics; useful additions to the labour force or a drain on housing and education. They bring with them a social and cultural identity, and it is often in the field of culture that the value of immigration is most powerfully expressed. In the twentieth century, as Terry Eagleton has reminded us,[1] the seven most important British writers have been a Pole, three Americans, two Irishmen and an Englishman: Joseph Conrad, Henry James, T.S. Eliot, Ezra Pound, W.B. Yeats, James Joyce and D.H. Lawrence. We need to remember that immigration has been a vital ingredient in the making of Britain and British culture, and that this 'green and pleasant land' was built up by periodical waves of immigrants, each making its special contribution to the common wealth of British cultural and social life.

One particular wave, however, the one that originated in the Commonwealth Caribbean during the second half of the twentieth century, radically affected the society's attitude to immigration and brought with it exceptional problems and persistent conflict and hostility. John F. Kennedy spoke proudly of the United States as 'a nation of immigrants'. To say that today about Britain might give offence, because the word 'immigrants' has been downgraded: it now conjures up, almost exclusively, dark strangers from an alien culture. But those Dark Arrivants from the Caribbean were not aliens. They were British migrant workers seeking jobs which they had been invited by the British government to fill. What should have been the most problem-free and so perhaps the most successful wave of immigration swiftly and ironically became the most problematic. To look for the reasons for this we need to consider the general history of British immigration.

Britain has always absorbed and drawn strength from immigration. The first settlers, the prehistoric peoples of the neolithic and bronze ages, were followed, during the Iron Age, by the Celts, a name that itself derives from their older name, 'Keltoi', meaning 'strangers' or 'outsiders'.[2] They were conquered by the Romans, who in turn were followed by the Jutes, Angles and Saxons. The later arrival of the Danes and Norwegians might also be seen ultimately as a kind of immigration although, at first sight, it hardly seems reasonable to speak like this about the notorious Vikings. Their arrival was certainly violent and dramatic. They plundered and raped, but they settled, adding their own vigour and initiative to British life and culture. It is true that these Nordic arrivals were related to the earlier Anglo-Saxons; different branches, one might say, of one family of Teutonic origin, but in today's Britain, Teutonic blue eye-colour and flaxen hair represent a recessive gene. The dominant type is represented by brown eyes and hair, the earlier, Celtic-Roman inheritance which was later reinforced by immigration from the warmer, southern climates; from France and the Mediterranean in particular.

Britain was colonised by France in the eleventh century. Edward the Confessor had a special kinship with Norman France. There were already many Normans holding important administrative positions in Britain. The Norman Conquest of 1066 therefore was, paradoxically, both a consolidation of Norman influence and the first incursion of truly alien immigrants. For with William of Normandy there came large numbers of people of very different temperament, native to the warm South; Bretons, Flemings, Picards, Burgundians. From their settlement came the development of the new industrial arts; cloth-making, weaving and dyeing, sheep-farming, masonry and stone-building. By the thirteenth century English cloth was being exported to Spain, and the famous wool trade of Flanders was being challenged by English wool. The commercial importance of Britain in the later Middle Ages was a magnet to alien immigrants seeking a favourable financial climate. Jews and Florentines had, by the beginning of the fourteenth century, been invited to act as bankers and general organisers of business transactions such as the collection of Papal revenues and the payment and transmission of accounts due. They were virtually the country's bankers and financiers. In fact, much of Britain's commercial life was run by aliens. It is thought, for example, that the weighing system of 'Avoir-Du-Pois' (still stubbornly used in Britain instead of the official decimal system) was adopted during the thirteenth century to please Spanish wool merchants. By the nineteenth century, this is how immigration came to be seen:

> The isolation of our country and the character of our people have been so marked, that we have been able to receive all sorts of strangers from abroad and to assimilate them; they have not remained as separate elements . . . they have been absorbed into our national life.[3]

In fact, the waves of alien immigrants, Lombards, Flemings, Italians and Jews, who came to Britain during the fourteenth century did cause resentment among native Britons. They were, after all, monopolising the country's economic power. The Flemings, for instance, had become successful bankers in London. A group of them were attacked at Southwark by an enraged mob. The miserable Flemings were forced to say the words 'bread and cheese'. Those who could not produce a London accent were summarily despatched. (That must surely be the earliest recorded use of a linguistic test of 'Britishness'.[4]) Jews, the first moneylenders, were disliked and often persecuted. Shakespeare's Shylock, remember, was not the merchant of Venice of the play's title; he was a moneylender. He would have been as familiar a figure to the Elizabethan audience as Fagin was to Victorian readers of Dickens's *Oliver Twist*: the Alien Immigrant in London. Anti-semitic rhetoric was vigorous right up to the early twentieth century. The Right Reverend Bishop of Stepney warned that: 'the East End of London is being swamped by aliens who are coming in like an army of locusts eating up the native population'.[5]

There is nothing new about hostility to aliens. The 'immigrant problem' has an ancient history. Each new wave of immigrants had to deal with the thorny problem of settlement. The Gascony merchants, Flemish weavers, Italian artisans, the Walloons, the Dutch and French Huguenots, all found the going tough. But in the end, all were able to blend into the cultural, social and political landscape: they became British, part of the face of a United Kingdom. Then the Dark Strangers came. The West Indian poet, Edward Kamau Brathwaite, in his ironically titled *Rights of Passage* looks at the dilemma of these Dark Arrivants:

Where then is the nigger's
home?

In Paris Brixton Kingston
Rome?

Here?
Or in Heaven?

What crime
his dark

dividing
skin is hiding?

What guilt
now drives him

on?
Will exile never

end? . . .

(Postlude/Home)

As Brathwaite's poem[6] suggests, the black migrant was as
emblematic as the Wandering Jew. Certainly the West Indian has
always been a migratory figure. The region was itself built up by the
migratory movements, first of the Aboriginal Indians, then of
Europeans followed by the forced migration of Africans and later
indentured whites and Asians. After Emancipation, migration was also
a means of escape from bondage to the land and, as a means of
finding work, migration became a traditional feature of Caribbean
life. Up to the 1880s, the same 'push' and 'pull' factors which create
international patterns of migration has operated within the region
itself. During the 1930s, for example, there was heavy migration from
overcrowded, economically depressed Barbados to land-rich, under-
populated British Guiana (Guyana). In the 1970s the reverse
movement took place; from economically and politically depressed
Guyana to relatively stable Barbados. During the depression of the
1930s, Trinidadians emigrated to oil-rich Venezuela, as later, in the
1970s, workers from poorer islands emigrated to the then oil-rich
Trinidad. As island economies faltered or grew, so they acted as 'push'
and 'pull' factors affecting migration between territories. But under-
development, scarcity of land, overcrowding, political repression and
so on, combined with the powerful 'pull' factors of opportunity for
employment and political freedom forced the migrant stream more
and more firmly towards the metropolitan countries.

In the first decade of the twentieth century, the Panama Canal project had provided work for large numbers of Caribbean migrants. Many thousands of West Indian islanders arrived to help in the digging of a canal that was to cost $300,000,000 and about 4000 West Indian lives from accident and disease. The canal had a profound effect both on Panama, which found itself a pawn to US interests, and on the Caribbean as a whole. The West Indian islands were no longer isolated, but on an important route of world commerce. The United States' interest in Caribbean security was bound up with the presence of the canal, which was opened in 1914, at the start of the First World War. US influence over the Caribbean grew as Britain's declined during the years leading up to the great depression of the 1930s. When the 1914–18 war broke out, many West Indians were 'imported' to work in munitions factories in Britain, but the migrant stream flowed mainly to the US, where there were no significant restrictions, and work was plentiful. With the US Immigration Act of 1924, this outlet dried to a trickle. After the outbreak of the Second World War, the stream again flowed towards Britain.

Great Britain was the centre of a world empire made up of a bewildering variety of peoples and cultures. She was the 'Mother Country' to millions of dark-skinned, English-speaking, colonial sons and daughters, for whom simply to go there was to achieve status. The idea of the empire had sunk deep. Black civil servants in the

10.1. Troops leaving Kingston, 1916

10.2. Second World War: advertisement encouraging West Indian workers to come to Britain

10.3. West Indian pilot, Second World War

10.4. New arrivals from the Caribbean in an air raid shelter near Clapham Common

islands saved up to travel to Britain on their long summer leave (designed for white expatriates). British foods and fashions were slavishly copied by the middle-class browns and blacks. The colonies looked outwards to Britain for guidance and example. The Caribbean landscape was only a kind of papier-mâché, a romantic backdrop for the adventures of movie buccaneers. The real landscapes lay elsewhere, in Britain and Europe. During the First World War thousands of West Indians volunteered to serve the empire. With the advent of the Second World War, West Indians again answered the call of duty.

Britain, needing manpower to keep the war factories running, started recruitment drives in the overseas Dominions and colonies.

Many thousands of West Indian workers joined the war effort in the shipbuilding yards and munitions factories; 200 skilled machine-shop workers came from Jamaica; 500 experienced loggers from British Honduras (now Belize) were commissioned to work in the Scottish forests under harsh conditions.[7] Many joined the Red Cross and other nursing services in spite of the persistence of a colour bar and overt racial prejudice. There were 'grow more food' campaigns at home. 'Victory gardens' to help the war effort were common in the West Indies during this period. Thousands of men and women volunteered to serve in the army and air force. Many died in battle and many won decorations for bravery in action. When the war ended, the need for cheap labour to keep industry going in war-damaged Britain could not be met from local resources. Recruitment of West Indians, themselves desperately in need of work, became the answer. Caribbean governments, worried by overpopulation and underemployment, used emigration as a safety valve. In the 1940s and 1950s they eagerly responded to the recruitment drives initiated by London Transport, the Association of British Hotels and restaurants and the National Service.

West Indian immigration was therefore a logical development, the first exercise of its kind planned by a British government in order to obtain cheap British migrant labour from overseas. In July 1948, the *Empire Windrush* brought 492 skilled and semi-skilled Jamaican workers: the first batch. The *Evening Standard*'s banner headline,

10.5. The *Empire Windrush* arrives

10.6. Advertisement for one of the 'lady boats'

'Welcome Home', gave no hint of the trouble that was to come. Most of the men were given jobs through the Brixton Labour Exchange, the nearest one to the empty air-raid shelter in Clapham where they were housed. Brixton was to become one of the first areas of black settlement. After the war and demobilisation, many blacks and Indians had settled permanently and had invested in small businesses of their own; grocery shops, restaurants and rented accommodation. They could now send for their families. The black community grew.

Within ten years West Indian immigration to Britain ceased to be the mainly private undertaking of migrants and their families. Travel agents, shipping companies and airlines became promoters of the new travel boom. In 1953, migrants could only travel on three ships (the 'lady' boats) which sailed three or four times a year. By 1960, there were thirteen ships making up to 40 sailings a year, and charter flights were available. Migration to Britain had become almost a common-place. So what went wrong? Why did this wave of immigration create such obdurate resistance and conflict? After all, 100,000 Poles had been recruited and had settled in Britain after the Second World War; and 130,000 Jews were finally assimilated successfully in spite of initial resentment and prejudice. More than 345,000 Europeans had emigrated to Britain between 1945 and 1947.[8]

Parallels have been drawn between the two major waves of immigration that took place between 1870 and 1970; the important periods of Jewish and West Indian immigration. The similarities are tempting. Both tended to be concentrated in urban ghettos; both were peculiarly identifiable by their appearance, speech and social habits. Both seemed to present a genetic threat. The prejudices shown against them were couched in the same, panicky language:

I say, let these Jews have an island to themselves and let them live on one another ... [they] live like rats in a hole – I cannot find words bad enough for them myself.[9]

Now compare this outburst by the secretary of the Smethick branch of the Birmingham Immigration Control Association in 1965, complaining about West Indians' alien habits:

But these people are ruining our town ... the houses are falling apart, and they have a very high rate of T.B. Their habits are pretty terrible. They use the front garden as a rubbish dump, and heaven knows what they do in the toilets.[10]

Councillor Finney, in a letter to the *Smethick Telephone* had been even more alarmist:

West Indians could in less than half a century outnumber us English, and with one man, one vote, they could do something Hitler couldn't do – take over this country.[11]

The 'West Indian problem', unlike the 'Jewish problem' seemed to have no redeeming virtues. The Jews rapidly established themselves as traders, confirming, by their industriousness, the Victorian, 'self-help' philosophy of Samuel Smiles.[12]

Even if we view the question from the most material standpoint, the British race must gain by this assimilation ... the Israelite is proving himself to be a regenerating force, and a most useful acquisition to our citizenship.[13]

In June 1987 the Tower Hamlets Environment Trust organised an exhibition celebrating the Jewish heritage of the East End, where most of the 130,000 Eastern European Jewish immigrants settled during the nineteenth century. It was a celebration of the success of Jewish assimilation. One report on this event spoke of the need for 'greater awareness of Jewish heritage among non-Jews'. In the same article, however, the Asian inhabitants, the new immigrant East Enders, are described in disparaging terms. The area is: 'thick with the smell of their cooking, overrun by their ragtrade, dominated by Bengali confectioners, sari shops, halal butchers.'[14] It sounds like the familiar rhetoric of prejudice. The fact is, when black and Asian West Indians began to arrive in significant numbers from the late 1940s and early 1950s, their assimilation was bedevilled by skin colour and by their low status as colonials. There is a sad irony in this, since they generally regarded their Britishness as a source of pride, and Britain as the Mecca of Opportunity. In V.S. Naipaul's *Miguel Street* the entire community in a run-down Trinidad suburb is amazed when young Elias finally manages to pass a colonial overseas examination. This exam was the minimum requirement for a decent job, and gave the official stamp of approval to a student's hope of further study.

> 'The boy is a genius', Titus Hoyt said.
> 'Which boy?' Errol asked.
> 'Elias'.
> 'What Elias do?'
> 'The boy gone and pass the Cambridge Senior School Certificate.'
> Hat whistled. 'The Cambridge Senior School Certificate?'
> Titus Hoyt smiled. 'That self. He get a third grade. His name go be in the papers tomorrow . . .'
> . . . Hat said, 'What you going to do now, Elias? Look for work?'
> Elias spat. 'Nah. I think I will write the exam again.'
> I said, 'but why?'
> 'I want a second grade.'
> We understood. He wanted to be a doctor.
> Elias sat down on the pavement, and said, 'yes, boy I think I go take that exam again, and this year I go be so good that this Mr. Cambridge go bawl when he read what I write for him.'
> We were silent in wonder.
> 'Is the litricher and poultry does beat me.'[15]

The image of London as the hub of the civilised world had been part of the colonial conditioning. The Trinidadian writer, Sam Selvon, captures something of that feeling in his novel, *The Lonely Londoners*:

> The changing of the seasons, the cold slicing winds, the falling leaves, sunlight on green grass, snow on the land, London particular . . . to have said; 'I walked on Waterloo Bridge', 'I rendezvoused at Charing Cross', . . . to say these things, to have lived these things, to have lived in the great city of London, centre of the world. . . . to write a casual letter home beginning: 'Last night in Trafalgar Square'. . . .[16]

A further irony lies in the fact that those migrant workers who arrived on the *Empire Windrush* in 1948 were part of a long history of black immigration to Britain, which probably began during the Middle Ages with the early trade routes between Europe and the Mediterranean. African gold, the occupation of Spain by the Moors of

Muslim Africa, and finally the 'black gold' of the slave trade, ensured a black presence in Britain. But this presence was compromised from the start by the nature of its conception: the black person was an article of domestic value, an item of trade, a commodity, expendable as earth. This is the heart of the problem: those twentieth-century arrivals still carried the stigmata of slavery exemplified by this sort of advertisement:

> To be sold. A pretty little Negro boy, about nine years old, and well limb'd. If not disposed of, is to be sent to the West Indies in six days' time. He is to be seen at the Dolphin Tavern in Tower street.[17]

In imperial Britain, as in the colonial West Indies, blacks were property; chattels conferring status on their owners and employers. They were fashionable in Elizabethan times, too. So many freed blacks settled in England that Queen Elizabeth issued two Royal Proclamations, one in 1596 and a second in 1601, ordering the expulsion of all 'negroes and blackamoors which are crept into this realm . . . to the

10.7. *The Family of Sir William Young* by Zoffany

10.8. Portrait of Ignatius Sancho by Gainsborough

great annoyance of her own leige people who want the relief which these people consume'. But the community of blacks kept growing. For one thing, they were part of the ostentatious wealth of the nobility, appearing in much the same role as their owners' fine dogs and horses.[18] There were outstanding black figures[19] who became respectable, and occasionally, respected, citizens. One was the Jamaican-born slave, Francis Barber, who was given his freedom in 1752 when his owner died. Francis became a servant to the famous Dr Samuel Johnson. When Johnson died, Francis inherited his property and an income of £70 a year. With his wife, Elizabeth, he established and ran a school near Lichfield in Staffordshire. He died in 1801. A former slave, Ignatius Sancho, was the protégé of the Duke and Duchess of Montagu. He was well read and something of a poet and dramatist. His portrait was painted by Gainsborough, and his friends included Lawrence Sterne, the writer, and the dramatist, David Garrick. Sancho married a black West Indian woman and ran a grocer's shop in Charles Street, Westminster. This 'poor blacky grocer', as he calls himself in his diary, had to face frequent insult and abuse because of his colour. Yet, after his death in poverty in 1780, his letters, in book form, went rapidly through five editions and added support to the anti-slavery movement.

   Blacks had been in Britain for centuries. In 1764, there had already been complaints about their numbers in London:

The practice of importing Negro servants into these kingdoms is said to be already a grievance that requires a remedy, and yet it is every day encouraged, insomuch that the number in this metropolis only is supposed to be near 20,000; the main objection is, that they cease to consider themselves as slaves in this free country, nor will they put up with an inequality of treatment, nor more willingly perform the laborious offices of servitude than our own people, and if put to do it, are generally sullen, spiteful, treacherous, and revengeful.[20]

An entirely understandable reaction, one might think, under the circumstances. The writer of the article then goes on to recommend the inoculation of horned cattle in Saxony as a means of reducing the mortality rate of the herds, another useful import. Of course, the West Indian immigrants who arrived in large numbers during the 1940s and 1950s were also, in a sense, imports. They, too, were expected to undertake those 'laborious offices' while putting up with 'inequality of treatment'. And in time they too were to appear 'sullen, spiteful . . . and revengeful'. In spite of everything, blacks became a part of British life, even if it was more often the low life of the ports and cities. There is, in fact, quite an impressive list of distinguished black immigrants.[21]

In the nineteenth century, a young Jamaican woman had been to the Crimea to help the wounded in the battlefield. She was at the battle of Tchernaya, the assault on Redan, and nursed the wounded at the fall of Sebastopol. Before that, she had spent three years nursing cholera victims in Panama. On her return to London in 1857 she was, like her white counterpart, Florence Nightingale, to became famous. Her name was Mary Seacole and she had left Jamaica to come to Britain to offer her services in the war effort. She finally had to pay her own way to the Crimea. Coloured nurses simply did not exist in the eyes of officialdom at that time. But the soldiers she had helped came to her aid when she returned, famous but poor. Nine military bands held a four-day festival (today, I suppose, we might call it 'nurse-Aid') to raise money for her. Mary Seacole died in 1881 and is buried at St Mary's Cemetery, Harrow Road, London.

Leary Constantine, a successful Test cricketer from Trinidad, decided to emigrate to Britain in 1929. He and his wife settled in Nelson, Lancashire, and he played in the Lancashire league as its team captain. He was well liked and widely respected. During the Second World War, the Ministry of Labour appointed him welfare officer for West Indians in Manchester. He became a barrister, wrote a book about colour discrimination (*The Colour Bar*, 1954), became high commissioner for Trinidad and Tobago and was knighted in 1962. He became a governor of the BBC and, in 1969, was made a life peer. Lord Constantine died in 1971.

Blacks not only settled in Britain but also married white Britons, adding to the heterogeneous nature of British society. John Archer, son of a West Indian father and an Irish mother, became the first coloured man in history to be elected mayor of an English borough. He was elected mayor of Battersea, London, in 1913. Samuel Coleridge-Taylor, the conductor and composer who is most remembered for his 'Hiawatha's Wedding Feast' and 'An African Suite', was born in Holborn in 1875, of an African father and an English mother. His father was a member of the Royal College of Surgeons. His daughter, Averil, also became a composer/conductor, and has conducted her father's music at the Royal Albert Hall.[22]

At the time of the 1951 census, 15,307 West Indians were living in Britain. By 1958 the figure estimated by the Migrant Services Division was 120,000. This was also a period of heavy immigration from the Indian subcontinent. By 1960 there were between 70,000 and 100,000 Indians and Pakistanis in Great Britain. Asian immigration was harder to estimate because there was no Migrant Services Division in their countries' High Commissions, and also because emigration had been a tradition taken virtually for granted. Before 1947 India had exported large numbers of its people to areas where they were needed as indentured and contract labour within the British Empire, including the West Indies. Independence in 1947 made little difference. After 1955 increasing numbers entered Britain looking for work. The Asian community of Bradford has now become so large and well-organised that the city advertises their cultural presence as part of an exotic tourist package. The Indian community, as one commentator put it, 'enlivens the Northern grit and Gothic'.

But such apparent successes remain recent and fragile, almost exotic by definition. The early migrants had to endure a double exile. As settlers in Britain, they were made to feel strangers, and they had, over the years, become strangers to the Caribbean they had left. Derek Walcott writes about the disillusioning return of the exile:

> Whatever else we learned
> at school, like solemn Afro-Greeks eager for grades,
> of Helen and the shades
> of borrowed ancestors,
> there are no rites
> for those who have returned . . .
> only this fish-gut reeking beach
> whose spindly, sugar-headed children race
> whose starved, pot-bellied children race

pelting up from the shallows
because your clothes,
your posture
seem a tourist's . . .
all this you knew,
but never guessed you'd come
to know there are homecomings without home.[23]

The 'Dark Arrivants' during the late 1950s were isolated and made to feel unwelcome. They were the 'Lonely Londoners': disillusionment began to set in, then resentment. One of the characters in Samuel Selvon's novel, an innocent called Gallahad, turned away by yet another landlady, philosophically addresses his black skin:

colour, is you that causing all this, you know. . . . I ain't do anything to infuriate the people and them, is you! look at you, you so black and innocent, and this time so, you causing misery all over the world.

He reports the discovery to his friend, Moses: 'Is not we the people don't like. Is the colour black.'[24]

The Lonely Londoners was published in 1956. Two years later, race riots exploded in Notting Hill and Nottingham city. The riots were

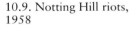

10.9. Notting Hill riots, 1958

the result of anti-black feeling. There were attacks on black people, many of whom were injured, and their property destroyed. The situation was so serious, that the *Daily Mirror* ran a series of articles to educate white readers. These articles offered to 'give people the facts about coloured people',[25] a belated attempt to expose the racist nature of commonly held fears about West Indian immigrants. Less than a year later, a West Indian carpenter, Kelso Cochrane, was stabbed to death on the streets of Notting Hill. It was during this period that two racist organisations, the White Defence League and the National Labour Party, came together as the British National Front. By the late 1960s and early 1970s 'Paki-bashing' and 'nigger-hunting' had become familiar phrases in the vocabulary of racial violence. Black retaliation only increased the conflict, precipitating sterner police action and further black resentment, hostility and urban insurrection, beginning in 1976 during the Notting Hill Carnival celebrations, and ending in 1985 with the Tottenham and Handsworth riots. In the summer of 1981, street fighting in London, Liverpool and Manchester went on for eight consecutive days. Today, there is greater tolerance and a growing awareness of the social and cultural contribution made by black immigrants and their descendants. But the opportunity for a smooth transition had been missed. When the Commonwealth Immigration Acts began to appear, from 1962 onwards, disillusionment had been followed by dismay. In spite of official denials to the contrary, race and immigration control were not separate issues. Immigration laws are always aimed at keeping out 'undesirables'. It soon became clear that black immigrants were undesirable.

Immigration control had begun in 1905 with the Aliens Act, aimed at émigré Jews from Eastern Europe. The Act was intended, in the words of a popular slogan, to keep out Aliens and keep Britain British. The later Acts followed the same spirit; the slogans changed to: 'keep out Blacks and keep Britain White'. The British government started to close the door on unrestricted entry with the Commonwealth Immigration Act of 1962, the first of many Acts designed to limit the influx of the Dark Strangers. In 1964, Peter Griffith, Conservative, won a bye-election over Labour's Patrick Gordon Walker. One of Griffith's slogans was: 'If you want a nigger for a neighbour, vote Liberal or Labour'.[26] There were votes to be won over immigration control. The new Labour government introduced a White Paper which compromised their earlier opposition to the Act. Roy Hattersley, MP, explained:

Without integration, limitation is inexcusable.
Without limitation, integration is impossible.[27]

10.10. Sign on lodgings banning 'coloureds'

Whatever that meant, it clearly acknowledged the link between immigration control and race. To black Britons, the idea of the family of the Commonwealth faded like an illusion. The 1968 Commonwealth Immigrants Act tightened control still further. Entry to the UK was no longer a right for Commonwealth citizens, especially if they came from the coloured Commonwealth. Passed in the Year of Human Rights, the Act was considered racially biased by the European Commission on Human Rights. One month after the Act was passed, Enoch Powell made his celebrated 'rivers of blood' speech in Birmingham. He was sacked from the Tory Shadow Cabinet, but received widespread popular support. In Sheffield, for instance, Indian and Pakistani restaurants had virtually every window broken.

Behind these Immigration Acts lay the wish to prevent racial conflict, but by tacitly acknowledging a colour bar, they served to encourage it. The problem was not 'overcrowding' or job competition. In most years since 1948, according to *Population Trends* (37, autumn 1984),[28] more people left than entered Britain. Even when there were no controls, immigration figures generally matched the figures for work opportunities. The effect of the controls had been to withdraw the right of immigration from black citizens of 'the United Kingdom and Colonies'.

There is still intolerance, prejudice and suspicion. The Dark Stranger is the eternal Other, different, a threat more imagined than real. In spite of the Race Relations Act, racial violence seems to be once again on the increase, and the black British community feels itself to be discriminated against even by the police. Today the descendants of those early immigrants are an indelible part of multiracial, multicultural Britain. Asian and West Indian cultural expression, its literature, art, food and music have added a distinctive flavour to the cultural life of Britain. Young black or Asian Britons easily pass the linguistic test of Britishness: the phrase 'bread and cheese' that had been the undoing of those hapless, immigrant Flemings in fourteenth-century London, is authentic in their mouths. In the landscape and culture of Britain they are insiders, but too often made to feel outsiders because of colour or race. The chance was missed to let that first wave of Dark Arrivants play their part in the making of Britain. For them, the journey ended (as one suspects it did for V.S. Naipaul) in an enigmatic arrival:

> A stranger here, with the nerves of a stranger, and yet with the knowledge of the language and the history of the language and the writing, I could find a special kind of past in what I saw . . . a landscape which . . . existed for me only in my heart. From that first spring I had known that such a moment was going to come. . . . And as at a death, everything here that had been a source of pleasure and surprise, everything that had welcomed me and healed me, became a cause for pain.[29]

The future, for the descendants of those 'Dark Strangers', will, one hopes, be different. They share in the making of Britain: perhaps they will not have to endure the pain of a 'homecoming without home'.

Further Reading

Banton (ed.), *White and Coloured* (Boston, 1976); Colin Brock (ed.), *The Caribbean in Europe* (London, 1986); Ann Dummett (ed.), *Towards a Just Immigration Policy* (London, 1986); Peter Fryer, *Staying Power. The History of Black People in Britain* (London, 1984); Griffith *et al.*, *Coloured Immigrants in Britain* (Oxford, 1960); Dilip Hiro, *Black British/White British* (London, 1971).

CHAPTER ELEVEN

A Prosperous People

Leslie Hannah

There are several million people alive today who were born in the first decade or so of the twentieth century. These 70 and 80 year olds seem to me to have had a pretty grim life. Two world wars, a world depression between them, and life on the old age pension now is not my idea of paradise. Yet when old people talk about their experiences, after sharing the inevitable nostalgia for the old days, they almost all agree that there have been vast improvements in living standards over the century as a whole: they see later generations as overwhelmingly more fortunate than themselves.[1] Material standards of living and the range of lifetime opportunities have both increased markedly in twentieth-century Britain, and this is true even for pensioners. The state old age pension now is worth three times as much in real terms as when it was first introduced in 1909. What is more, the chance of drawing it has greatly increased with the reduction in the pension age from 70 for all to 65 for men and 60 for women and with the conquest by modern drugs of killer diseases such as pneumonia and tuberculosis. The typical man retiring today also has an occupational pension. He is thus better off in real terms when retired than his parents would have been on a full manual worker's wage at the time he was born.[2]

Moreover, improvements in living standards are not confined to the retired. The real wages of manual workers have doubled about every 30 years so that each generation of workers has been substantially better off than its predecessors.[3] Working-class budgets used to be dominated by essentials such as food, clothing and housing. Nowadays there is a much wider variety of spending on things like televisions or holidays abroad, many of which simply were not available at the beginning of the century.

Workers have chosen to take their increased living standards not

11.1. At the seaside, 1940s

11.2. A family holiday in Marbella

just in improved spending power but also in greater leisure. Whereas 60 hours a week was the norm at the beginning of the century, 40 hours a week is in many industries now the maximum; and Saturday working, once a must for almost everyone, is now considered an 'unsocial hour'. Workers were then lucky to be paid at all for a one-week annual holiday in the local seaside resort by train or charabanc; now the worker who does not take four weeks paid holiday a year, at least one or two of them in faraway places with guaranteed sunshine, is unlucky.[4]

For some people this increase in leisure has been at the cost of an increased pace of labour during working hours. But generally mechanisation and improved methods have greatly reduced the sheer toil of the working day: cranes and containers have superseded the docker's back, automatic cutters and loaders have replaced the coal miner's pick and shovel; and everywhere computerisation and automation — and more recently robotisation — have replaced some of the heavy or boring jobs once performed by people.

The twentieth-century improvement of ordinary people's living standards is largely a result of such improvements in efficiency in the economy overall. Most people are wealthier because the national cake is bigger: our productive power and efficiency is so much greater than it was at the beginning of the century. But some of the improvement comes from the twentieth-century pressures for sharing the national cake more equally.[5] At the beginning of the century Britain was not in the modern sense a democracy: the majority of working-class people did not vote. But when poorer workers and women got the vote in 1918 and the Labour Party became both the major opposition party and a realistic alternative government, the long political struggle for redistribution went into higher gear. This struggle has perhaps been at its most effective in widening educational opportunity, particularly at the secondary and higher levels. Where once secondary schools and universities were closed except to a few scholarship boys and those who could afford to pay, there is, for all our grumbles about the present educational system's remaining shortcomings, now much more real equality of opportunity. And the proportion of jobs in the economy requiring significant education and training has greatly increased while jobs requiring just the brute force of the labourer are in decline.

Redistribution has not been confined to educational opportunity. There are also now important financial transfers from wealthier people through taxes to the poorer ones receiving payments from the welfare state. Even poorer families can now plan their spending in the secure knowledge that there is an income floor provided by social security in times of sickness, unemployment or old age. Debates about

11.3. Schoolyard at the end of the nineteenth century

11.4. A modern classroom

redistribution have often held the centre of the political stage. Yet if you look at the impact of this redistribution on living standards, the effects have been small relative to the power of growing productivity in the economy as a whole. The average worker of 1900, for example, certainly could not aspire to own a car, but nowadays the average worker would expect to drive perhaps three second-hand and three new cars in the course of his working life. There has clearly been a vast improvement in living standards: but more than five of the cars have come to him through improved productivity, and only a small proportion – perhaps four wheels and an engine – of the sixth car comes from the extra income he gets as a result of redistribution from the rich to the poor.

Shares of income and wealth are more equal than they were at the beginning of the century, but because everyone has been getting better off, the pressure for redistribution has been less than many of the rich earlier feared. It is harder to resent others being better off if you are getting better off all the time yourself, and if your children can aspire to an even better life that is all the more likely to make you accept the inequalities of class barriers that remain. It is very difficult indeed for more than a few working-class children in any school to aspire to becoming members of the wealthy establishment and Britain still has one of the most class-ridden societies in the advanced industrial world. But many working-class children *can* aspire to a more comfortable life in a middle-class occupation won by education. These upwardly mobile groups are among the staunchest supporters of the status quo. Even when class barriers – or barriers of gender prejudice or race prejudice – restrict entry to certain white-collar groups, our society offers to the lucky few the entrepreneurial route to wealth and influence. The competitive markets of capitalism are colour blind and gender blind: if you can build a better mousetrap no one cares much who you are, they care about what you can do for them, and they beat a path to your door. It is not surprising, then, that some of the most underprivileged groups of the late nineteenth century have taken the entrepreneurial route to present-day economic success, many of them making fortunes; retailing or property appear to be particularly inviting to newcomers. The Jews of the early part of this century who were barrow boys or sweatshop workers in the clothing industry when their families arrived penniless in Britain, fleeing from the pogroms on the continent, are the supermarket kings of today. The Asian businessmen who fled from their oppressors in Africa are now repeating that process.

While our mobile society has enabled the most skilled and restless entrepreneurs to come to terms with inequality by coming out on top, this process of economic growth has not been costless for the more passive participants. The economic changes and efficiency increases of the twentieth century have required tremendous flexibility from the population as a whole.[6] The centre of industrial activity has moved away from the shipyards of the Tyne and the Clyde and from the cotton mills of Lancashire towards the modern factory estates of the South East and the knowledge-based high-tech centres of Silicon Glen in Scotland or Silicon Fen around Cambridge. This has meant a lot of people 'getting on yer bike' and uprooting their homes and families to move to where the jobs are. The pace of change and the redundancy of old skills, have, if anything, been more rapid than in the nineteenth century. This process does not give a satisfactory life to everyone, and the transition problems caused by these massive structural changes can be painful. Mass unemployment came to Britain in the 1930s as the world economic slump drained our export industries of jobs. The oil crisis of 1973 and the squeeze of Mrs Thatcher's new economic policy have again more recently heightened the distress of the millions without jobs. More generally, even when employment prospects have not been so dire, fears have been expressed that machines will take over from men, and make such conditions of mass unemployment permanent. The spectre of the 1930s dole queues for long paralysed labour markets in Britain, and encouraged the growth of restrictive practices designed to protect workers from unemployment. But workers have usually succeeded only in temporarily stemming the economic and technological forces they seek to hold back. There were once more than a million coal miners in Britain, whereas now British Coal numbers its employees only in tens of thousands. We may like to blame this decline on the workforce or Arthur Scargill or Ian MacGregor, according to political taste, but the real reason is more prosaic: it is because as householders we prefer to buy cheaper, more convenient or more efficient fuels than coal and our industrialists in their factories make much the same choices. Workers have only rarely been successful for very long periods in resisting technological and market changes: and even the few who have, like the overpaid and unloved print workers, have now succumbed to a completely new technology which simply bypassed them. The workers who have done best out of modern capitalism by contrast are those who have acquired new skills, moved to new factories and shown the flexibility which constant efficiency increases require. Nowadays the redundancy of old skills and the need to acquire new ones poses even greater strains than in the nineteenth century. Yet, as a richer society we are in the twentieth century perhaps better able to handle them more humanely and considerately. Retraining grants, unemployment benefit, and redundancy payments are all quite new ways in which twentieth-century society has accepted that those who suffer most

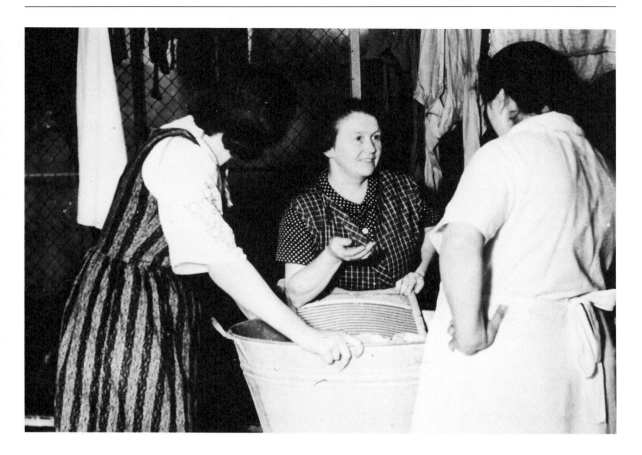

11.5. Washday at the public laundry

from the change should reap some of the benefits. Perhaps for that reason alone the changes required have been more readily accepted by the population than the upheavals of the nineteenth.

The most visible sign of twentieth-century economic growth is, of course, the consumer revolution, embodied most obviously in the consumer durables such as cars and washing machines which formed no part of working people's budgets in 1900 but now take up a large part. Indeed many things that we now take for granted would have amazed our great-grandparents. At the end of Queen Victoria's reign only one or two houses in a hundred had electricity – not surprisingly because just to buy the electricity to keep half a dozen bulbs lit at night then cost more than many workers' weekly earnings. Now the availability of cheap electricity brings flexible power to every home. Washing machines, for example, have reduced to ten minutes' light work what used to take many housewives a full Monday of heavy toil.[7] No less important in improving the home environment in the present century has been the general introduction into ordinary people's homes of hot and cold running water, inside lavatories and

11.6. Scrubbing the linoleum

central heating; and the spreading use of easy care fabrics, stainless steel cutlery and new cleaning materials has greatly reduced the drudgery of housework. (Smaller family size has also reduced the time housewives are tied down to drudgery in the home.) Those who stay at home – not only the workers in factories – have, then, also had greatly increased leisure time.

Many of these consumer innovations require investments in consumer durables which would have been impossible for individual families to afford at the earnings levels of 1900. Even for richer workers of the day such as miners or cotton spinners, who could afford to spend more, credit for large purchases was then difficult to obtain. Most working-class families would rely on the pawnbroker – charging punitive interest rates – when they needed cash, or hope for luck in gambling if they needed to finance a major purchase.[8] I remember puzzling for a long time over why, in the 1920s, so few people bought the new-fangled vacuum cleaners when they were such obviously useful gadgets. The problem was not that they could not afford the £5 which Hoovers then cost. It was simply that they could not afford the carpets, which were then a luxury for working-class families. They had to make do with the oilcloth and lino which could as easily be cleaned by traditional methods. Nowadays, by contrast, even capital expenditures as large as a car can be financed by most families through hire purchase, charge accounts or credit cards at interest rates which are considerably less usurious than those demanded of working-class borrowers at the beginning of the century. The biggest expenditure most people undertake is buying a house. At

11.7. The 1926 vacuum
cleaner

11.8. Post-war house building for a new generation of home-owners

the beginning of the century perhaps only one in ten people owned their own houses, and most people rented; now the proportion owning their own house is around two-thirds. By 1986 there was more than £150bn of outstanding loans for house purchase. And other credit has also mushroomed: there was more than £30bn outstanding at the end of last year, more than £5bn of it on credit cards. But credit is not purely a one-sided bubble, people are now accumulating more savings – which give them both income and flexibility – than ever before.

The twentieth-century economic experience has, then, been a history of superlatives. All the statistics on income, leisure, spending or saving suggest that the British are not only better off than ever before, but for most of the time since the Second World War have been getting better off *faster* than ever before. These improvements in living standards are not the preserve of one group but have been spread widely throughout society. Yet people appear to have been dissatisfied by their achievements in this age of affluence. The talk for many decades now has been of British economic decline, and of 'the British disease': an abiding whiff of failure surrounds most people's perceptions of our twentieth-century experience.[9]

The explanation of this paradox lies not in the statistics of spending and growth but in the psychology of expectations. It is not just the reality of how much they can save and spend that affects people's satisfaction but also how that reality compares with their expectations. The twentieth century has seen not just the consumer revolution and the breakthrough to the age of affluence but an even more remarkable revolution of rising expectations. That is why the overwhelming impression of old people, even now the post-war boom has faded with the return of unemployment, is that the younger generation are spoilt, and that they are far luckier than they will admit to being.

Consider the perceptions of the generation which was born in the first decade of the century. When they were young, their parents' wages grew only slowly year by year, if at all. When they themselves were old enough to join the workforce, they encountered the mass unemployment of the inter-war years, rising by 1932 to a record high level. When recovery came in the war, it was a recovery of jobs but for more than a decade of war and post-war austerity, food, clothes and other consumer goods were in desperately short supply. By contrast, the last twenty years of their working life from the 1950s to the early 1970s, must have seemed a golden age of rising affluence and new opportunity; and their children also grew up with the expectation of that continuing. The crash of 1973 was, then, a bitter harvest for them to reap, and one they were ill prepared to take as the children of the age of affluence.

But the major modern source of discontent with our economic performance has not really been with the higher levels of prosperity which we attained and the temporary setbacks of recent years. Rather it was the sense that, while we might have done well, others had done better. It may be that in the great post-war boom our growth rate of 2 or 3 per cent a year was better than we had ever attained before, but it looked less impressive in a period when some other major industrial countries were attaining levels of 5 per cent or more.[10] Moreover, the evidence shows that, far from being a purely post-war phenomenon, Britain's poor relative performance goes back for at least a hundred years. For almost the whole of that period, decade by decade Britain has been growing at only a half or less the rate achieved on average by countries such as the USA, Japan, Germany, France or Italy. A few percentage points difference may not amount to much in the short term, and Britain began with a large lead over most of these countries in the *level* of her living standards. Yet the inexorable power of growth rates compounded year by year takes its toll eventually. The French and Germans overtook us in the 1960s, the Italians and the Japanese more recently.[11]

The reason is not that they have done things very differently from us; it is often simply that they have done more of it — and perhaps done it better — than us. The changes I have described are very much the changes which these other societies have also undergone. Japan has seen the decline of its textile and shipbuilding industries, America and Germany have seen the rise of electrification and mechanisation in the factory and in the home. The populations of all these countries have grown better off and taken more leisure. But the bottom line is that in terms of productive efficiency the improvements abroad have gone farther than in Britain. This is most obviously visible in traded goods: the proliferation of imported cars on the English roads has made our declining industrial powers plain for all to see.[12] But changes in leisure and services have also meant that British workers – who in 1900 would hardly have paused to compare themselves to German or American workers for longer than they would have compared themselves to the natives of Timbuctoo – now see the contrasts in standards on television or on the Mediterranean beaches in the summer.

Britain is not, of course, the only country to have experienced a sense of shock and failure when brought up in this way against the brute facts of inferiority. For many countries the sense of shock was more profound and instantaneous: as when Japan and Germany faced the humiliation of military defeat in 1945 and the resulting economic dislocation and distress. Our economic failure is perhaps less palpable than theirs then, but their history suggests that countries can react psychologically to such stress by improving their performance.

Economists in the twentieth century have not unlocked the great mystery of why some countries are wealthier than others, and historians have done no better. What most students of these issues do agree on is that cultural, political, social and psychological factors probably have at least as much to do with it as economic ones. The last hundred years of continuously improving living standards are not in any absolute sense a failure. Yet it may be that our failure relative to the achievements of others is now giving Britain a jolt from which it will emerge as a very different society – and perhaps a more successful economy – than that which this century has seen so far.

Further Reading

Margaret Ackrill, *Manufacturing Industry since 1870* (Oxford, 1987); G.C. Allen, *The British Disease: a short essay on the nature and causes of the nation's lagging wealth*, 2nd edn, Hobart Paper: 67 (London, 1979); William Ashworth, *An Economic History of England 1870–1939* (London, 1960); Leslie Hannah, *The Rise of the Corporate Economy*, 2nd edn (London, 1983); Sidney Pollard, *The Development of the British Economy: 1914–1980*, 3rd edn (London, 1983); John F. Wright, *Britain in the Age of Economic Management: an economic history since 1939* (Oxford, 1979).

CHAPTER TWELVE

In the Shadow of the Past

Michael Ignatieff

However difficult, however foolish the enterprise may be, we can never resist trying to predict the future. Even though we ought to know better, we are all incorrigible crystal ball gazers. We want history to tell us not only how it was, but how it is going to be. But how are we to distinguish between short-term episodes — the media event — and long-term historical change? All we can say is that the more deeply rooted in the past a trend is, the more likely it is to continue in the future. Hence the sharper our historical sense, the more accurate our predictions are likely to be.

Even so, the future is sure to escape our grasp. Could anyone in 1945 have predicted what Britain would look like in the 1980s? A mid-sized power, divested of her empire and tied to Europe rather than to her former colonies? A manufacturing nation painfully struggling into a post-industrial future? A multiracial culture? A society of consumers rather than a society of classes? No one came close to predicting all this in 1945. If our parents failed to predict our world, we ought to be modest about imagining the world we will leave our children.

Visions of the future are actually snapshots of the present. Our predictions are likely to tell future generations more about *us* than they do about *them*. George Orwell's 1984 was much more about 1948 — shortages, bomb sites, rationing, war exhaustion and fear of Soviet totalitarianism — than about the sleek and anxious world of 1984.

What it means to be British has also changed beyond recognition since 1945. Britishness, above all, is a concept used to describe how the classes define themselves and how they get on together. In the classic films of the late 1940s and early 1950s — from *Brief Encounter* to *The Lavender Hill Mob* or *Passport to Pimlico* — this vanished self-idealisation was on display: a cocky and comic working class;

fumbling but endearing aristocrats and a practical, provincial middle class running the show; a world of dim but kindly policemen, cosy landladies, ridiculous toffs; a society held together by forbearance towards each other's eccentricities and a shared belief in Britain as the workshop of the world, as home of liberty and as defender of Europe against Hitler. Like all self-idealisations, this one was plausible to the degree that it was true and appealing to the degree that it ignored what the British preferred to forget: colonial rule overseas, overwork and underpay at home and increasing subservience to America as master of the world. These self-idealisations changed in the 1950s, as the locus of these films shifted from London and the Home Counties to the industrial North and as the working-class characters discovered their anger, and middle-class characters discovered their anguish. Yet the class compartments of British society remained as closed as before. Now in the 1980s, the situation is ambiguous: the compartments are open to those with luck, brains or money; people think of themselves less and less in class terms; and yet new patterns of exclusion have emerged, on racial, sexual and geographic lines, which continue to frustrate the possibility of a genuinely open and egalitarian society. In this situation, what it means to be British is unclear: the old language of class no longer applies and no new language of self-description has yet taken its place. The increasingly placeless styles of modern consumption add to the difficulty of defining what it means to be British. Today film and television are more likely to offer the British images of Los Angeles than images of London. The good life is sold to us from Japan or America and so images of our reality back home often suffer by comparison. Those films which do offer images of Britishness – *Letter to Brehznev*, *Mona Lisa*, *My Beautiful Laundrette* – paint a picture of a society multiracial and conflictual to a degree unimaginable in 1945. They also portray characters who are no longer content to express their roles as social types but are struggling either to define their social place or to escape from it. If the archetypal world of film is any guide, individuals are more ironical, suspicious or doubtful about their social identities as members of British society than they ever were in our parents' generation. Britishness in the 1980s has ceased to be an identity to be celebrated and has become one to be re-created or contested. The dominant national self-image is of division: race against race, region against region, rich against poor, yet these divisions are less a matter of pride and local identification and ever more a source of alienation.

If the very idea of what it means to be British has changed since 1945 how can we possibly imagine the changes that will engulf our children in the year 2000? In thinking about their future, we have to struggle not only to understand the changes within our own lifetime,

12.1. *The Lavender Hill
Mob*

12.2. *A Kind of Loving*

12.3. *Mona Lisa*

12.4. *My Beautiful Laundrette*

but also to master the fear which any contemplation of the future always evokes.

Thinking about the future has always aroused anxiety. For the people of 987 the approach of the year 1000 was an occasion for foreboding. A thousand years later, we approach the turn of a second millennium like frightened children crawling through a culvert. Yet this anxiety is paradoxical. By the measures that count — life expectancy, infant mortality, real income, possessions and social entitlements — the world of 1987 has realised many of the dreams of the 1945 era. Most of us live as well or better than our parents, yet relative inequalities between classes, regions and racial groups remain and are as keenly felt as absolute deprivations. Prosperity has been purchased at a price: destruction of nature, pollution and unforeseen levels of inter-personal violence. History's most sustained period of progress has resulted in a crisis of confidence in the idea of progress itself. The generation of 1945 was heir to a century of liberal, radical and socialist dreams of progress through planning and government intervention. When Truman Democrats, Gaullist republicans, Adenauerian conservatives and Attlee Labourites talked about the future in 1945, they evoked a vision of politics working hand in hand with science and technology to conquer disease, improve production and increase our mastery over nature. It is impossible for us to return to that world of assumptions now.

Above all else, history since 1945 has been dominated by the Bomb. No amount of argument about the rationality of deterrence has managed to reduce public anxiety about the nuclear arsenals of either side. Star Wars and zero option scenarios of a future beyond nuclear weapons speak eloquently to this generation's longing to escape from the weight of doom. Yet we live with the Bomb as we live with our own mortality, fortunately disbelieving in both. Even if substantial measures of nuclear disarmament occur, the possibility of global annihilation will still remain. What has once been invented cannot be forgotten. The cloud we began living under in August 1945 we are certain to pass onto our children.

Our faith in the powers of science and technology has not been lost, but Hiroshima, Minamata, Three Mile Island, Chernobyl have taught us to look for the hidden costs of science that we or our children are likely to pay. Likewise our faith in politics has taken a battering from the refusal of inequalities — in housing, education and employment — to respond to social democratic good intentions; and also from the tendency of good intentions to entail bad consequences — like the council house tower block. These doubts have particularly troubled socialist and social democratic heirs of the dreams of 1945. For conservatives, the future looks brighter if only because they are prepared, in theory at least, to let the market get on with its work of creative destruction. A consistent market conservative says of the future: Rejoice, rejoice, ye have no choice. In practice, however, no conservative can be seen to let the future take care of itself. The idea that government can and should master change is the most basic of any electorate's expectations: market conservatives defy this expectation at their peril. Yet it is an expectation which the sheer difficulty of anticipating the future, let alone planning for it, makes difficult for any government to satisfy.

In the British context, faith in the capacity of politics to master the future has been eroded above all by the rhetoric of decline which has seeped into all British political discussion. Indeed, this rhetoric has become the single greatest obstacle to thinking straight about the future.

We are in decline, it is said, because we have lost an empire; we are in decline because a once homogeneous and white society is now menaced by the hatreds and envies of the multiracial city; we are in decline because we no longer manufacture as many goods as we import; we are in decline because we cannot afford the social and cultural services that ought to define a civilised society, and so on. Once decline is accepted as the organising term for understanding the present, it becomes an easy matter to predict that we shall go on declining either into shabby English gentility or into Clockwork Orange dissolution.

Certainly Britain has failed to keep pace with the economic growth of her European neighbours, and more to the point, has failed to keep pace with her own expectations. In particular her social spending has failed to keep pace with the demands of the electorate for improvements in the public services that make up such a crucial component of the standard of living. In the face of slow growth relative to expectation, the corporatist bargain of British politics – the centrist consensus between government, management and labour known as Butskellism – slowly eroded and finally collapsed in the 1970s. Yet slow growth relative to one's neighbours is not the same thing as decline: much of the British population experienced a dramatic and sustained improvement in their standard of living during the 40 years after the war.

Much of the rhetoric of decline turns out, on closer examination, to be little more than pointless nostalgia. Those who regret the loss of empire wish to turn the clock back on the struggle against colonialism and imperialism throughout the third world. Yet the struggle in the colonies was in the name of values the British themselves invented. Either the values of democracy and self-government are universal or they are not; if universal, they entitle former colonial peoples to rule

12.5. Merthyr Tydfyl
1950s

themselves. The fact that few of the new post-colonial states are functioning democracies does not invalidate the principles which justified their emancipation from colonial rule. The fact that Britain did cede colonial independence in most cases before it had to be wrested in wars of liberation should be a matter of congratulation rather than shame. Loss of empire is not a symptom of decline: it is, on the contrary, a sign of progress.

Likewise, nostalgia for the supposed civilities of pre-war England forgets the degree to which civility reposed on fear and on what Ernest Bevin once called the 'poverty of desire' among the working classes. If contemporary English society is less civil, it is also more free. We cannot have one without the other.

If the right laments the grandeur and civility of imperial Britain, the left laments the shabby state of the social services and the decay of traditional working-class solidarity. Yet is it not possible that the symptoms of decline in public services — especially overcrowding and waiting lists — are a problem of success rather than failure, a sign of a system failing to keep pace with the demand which its own achievement has generated? Likewise, the laments for the decline of the old working class neglect the extent to which its certainties were those of a white, skilled, male elite, now out of touch with the new realities of a multiracial, feminist culture.

Any analysis of Britain's future place has to struggle free of the nostalgia which bedevils contemporary social judgements about Britain's present, whether from left or right. So what should we put in place of decline? Within what framework of assumptions about the world should we locate Britain's role in the future?

The first assumption is that we are already living in a global economy, dominated by large multinational corporations. Already most of us are working – as subcontractors, as freelanceers or as direct employees – for relatively few giant conglomerates, only a few of which are owned in Britain. Not many of us are making things: most of us are processing information or serving others and those of us who do best at it will be those with the most imaginative and daring use of technical knowledge. These trends should be embraced rather than resisted: those who say there will not be enough jobs to go around are underestimating the demand for skill and ingenuity. No one could have predicted the shrinkage of agricultural employment in the developed world in this century or could have imagined that there would be more than enough jobs in manufacturing and services to provide worthwhile work for people coming off the land. Likewise, no one can predict the eventual shape of the post-industrial employment that is already replacing jobs in manufacturing and the basic industries. But if we invest adequately in education and training, there is no reason to imagine a future in which work will be distributed only to the brainy few and denied the marginalised many.

The second assumption is that politically we will be living in a post-imperial world system in which the United States will lose its post-war hegemony in the face of the European Common Market and the industrialising nations of the Pacific Rim led by Japan. A free world without an all-dominant United States is a less secure place, a place in which Britain's role becomes more, not less, important. But it is also a world in which Britain faces challenges, particularly from the revolutionary and fundamentalist movements of the third world, which will present a constant threat to its markets and its domestic tranquillity.

The third assumption is that unless very radical economic reform occurs in the Soviet system and unless that reform encompasses relaxation of the party dictatorship over the society, the communist world will become increasingly backward and with that backwardness increasingly militarised and defensive. Without radical change in the Soviet bloc, therefore, there is no envisageable reduction in the proportion of their income western economies will have to devote to military expenditure. In other words, the margins of what is possible in domestic British politics will continue to be defined largely outside our borders, especially in the Soviet empire. The fourth assumption is that in this emerging global economy, the nation state as such will have increasing difficulty preserving its comparative advantages over its neighbours. Where capital and product markets are global, where innovations in one national economy are instantly copied in another, no national economy is immune from the pressures of global competition. It follows that the nation state's political control over its economy will be reduced; such control as Britain can exercise over her economy she will do so increasingly through her participation in huge trading blocs like the EEC. The days, if ever there were, when a Chancellor of the Exchequer's budget speech set the rules of the economic game for the country are clearly over. Yet the day of effective political management of the global economy has not yet arrived and the risks of our present interregnum – rising indebtedness in the third world, protectionism and trade wars in the developed world – cannot go on unaddressed. As Bette Davis used to say, 'Fasten your seat belts, boys, we're in for a bumpy ride'.

It is often said that the competition Britain has most to fear will come from the third world, from the low-wage export platforms of Pacific Asia. There is undoubted truth in this, but let us not forget the enormous accumulated advantages of developed societies such as Britain. Over two centuries ago, Adam Smith predicted that high-wage, high-skill economies as in Britain would always be able to compete with low-wage, low-skill economies by progressively abandoning simple products to poor countries and concentrating its own production on high-value, high-skill products. This constant process of moving up the ladder of goods towards the most valuable and leaving the least valuable to poorer countries is both a mechanism for the developed nations to remain rich and for the poorer nations to climb towards development.

If movements of money are becoming more international, so too are movements of people. After the burst of immigration from the third world into the developed world in the 1960s and 1970s the developed world imposed stringent immigration controls to hold onto its advantages. More and more people from the third world are using immigration as their private solution to the world's inequalities of resources. The developed world is going to have to chose between sharing world resources more fairly and admitting a regulated stream of third world immigration or fortifying its borders with the chainlink fences, dogs and helicopter patrols already to be seen on the border between Hong Kong and China and between the United States and Mexico.

In Britain, the future is here already: our cities are multiethnic communities, and the distribution of political power and social influence will have to adjust accordingly. Most of all, society's cultural self-image of what it means to be British will have to change. White

12.6. Multiracial
Britain: an
anti-apartheid
demonstration

Britain still accepts these facts grudgingly, but in a global perspective
the disgrace and consequent collapse of all forms of racial exclusiveness
and privilege is the greatest historical achievement of the post-war
period. For all the bitterness of our recent racial history, Britain has
reason to be hopeful: we have not created a guest worker proletariat
as in France or Germany, but a multiracial society of citizens. The
generation that will lead this country in the next century has grown up
taking a multiracial society for granted. The institutions of society
simply must catch up with the way that generation already feels about
race.

   Within this international context, what kind of British social order
can we envisage? The movement away from deference, discipline and
class privilege towards more competitive, envious, and individualistic
patterns of social striving is unstoppable. No one can be delighted
with the costs: rising divorce rates, crime and social violence, but we
easily forget the benefits: increased personal freedom and expressive-
ness. Britain's experience of violence, disorder and criminality since
1945 is more or less typical of the experience of the developed world.

It seems inevitable that the Britain of the year 2000 will be *both* more violent and more fiercely gripped by the dream of living one's life as one chooses.

Individualism is much condemned, of course, but the social movements which have changed Britain for the better in the past 15 years — feminism, black civil rights, gay liberation — have been

12.7. Pro-abortion demonstration

collective expressions of an individualist credo: let me be what I want to be; stop using my gender, my race or my sexual orientation to deny me the right to live my life as I choose.

What will tie a society of competitive individualists together? Provided, and it is a big if, the economic system can deliver on the society's advertised promises, there is no problem of stability. Modern societies do not lack for healing and integrating rituals: the monarchy enacts an affecting and uniting family soap opera in endless episodes as well as providing a vital symbolisation of constitutional continuity. Mass consumption and mass leisure patterns bind individuals together in common experience; the mass media provide the shared information on which the rules of the social game are based. Modern society is violent, crime-ridden and inescapably divided about its values but it is also stable, as early modern and developing societies were not. It is nostalgic to lament the disappearance of shared attachment to Britishness, to common values, to common civilities. What one person decries as a society in constant conflict with itself, another can praise just as plausibly, as a society that is free, because it debates and argues its future.

In this international context of ever more competitive, ever more individualistic societies, Britain can only claim that it is uniquely disadvantaged if it continues to lament the good old days when it ruled the waves. In fact its position is neither more nor less difficult than that of any European country. The advantages that gave Britain the lead in the Industrial Revolution have not disappeared: enviable natural resources, geographical compactness, special expertise in banking and insurance, a skilled labour force. She still enjoys the crucial cultural preconditions for economic success: political cohesion and social stability, relative freedom from regional or linguistic conflicts; a powerful tradition of respect for learning and invention; and widely diffused scientific and technical literacy.

The problem is not that Britain does not have powerful assets: it is that they are increasingly shared by her competitors.

British imperial insularity long cushioned this society from invidious comparisons: the British are not a people to take envious sideways glances at others: this is a good thing, because it speaks of a good deal of pride and self-contentment, but it also has a negative side, provincial snobbery. If there is any cultural attribute that spells economic death in the modern world it is provincial self-contentment, unwillingness to learn from others. Thus, the British like to think that they invented the welfare state and enjoy the most generous social provision in Europe. This was believable until the early 1960s. Since then, social welfare provision in Germany, Scandinavia and France has left Britain behind and the gap between British health statistics and Continental ones is growing. Likewise in the fields of education and job retraining.

Britain's entry into the European Economic Community began the shock treatment of invidious comparison with her European partners. Instead of congratulating themselves on the fact that they live somewhat better than their parents, and a lot better than their grandparents, increasing numbers of British people realise they do not live as well as their European neighbours. Standards of comparison, in other words, have become international rather than intergenerational. All over the developed world, this same process is occurring: ordinary people are more aware of the quality of other people's lives, more aware of relative differences between their standard of living and that of others – and this awareness is in itself a powerful impetus towards improving economic performance. It has penetrated the consciousness of almost everyone in the developed world that there is no such thing as a free lunch: those economies which do not learn from their neighbours, do not struggle constantly to improve themselves, will fall behind. Britain is not free to set its own genteel pace at the back of the pack, because as it falls farther behind its standard will fall not only relatively but absolutely.

Even predicting the next five years of British history is hard. Is the current period of renewed economic growth just an oil-fed blaze that will die out in a puff of smoke when the oil from the North Sea runs out? Or is Britain actually managing, slowly and painfully, to replace its reliance on old industries – coal, steel, textiles – with new ones – computers, biotechnology, financial services? If this shift towards a post-industrial economy is occurring, is it occurring fast enough to provide Britain with the export earnings necessary to cover its imports when oil revenues begin to decline in the next century? Is this new economy going to provide enough jobs for our children to do and enough wealth to provide for those who do not work?

The answers to these and nearly every other question Britain asks about its future depend on how it chooses to educate its children today. Education is the most powerful lever of aspiration and innovation. Education teaches discontent: it shows up the poverty of inherited desires and aspirations and as such is a solvent of the resignation and defeatism that prevents those at the bottom of a class society from fully believing in themselves or their children's chances. Of all the features that need to change in British society this is the most important: the deep reservoirs of silent resignation and defeatism that continue to prevent working-class children from believing that they can live better than their parents. There is no education capable of preparing a people for tomorrow: many of the jobs we are struggling to train people for today did not even exist ten years ago, and the same is even more likely to be true in the year 2000. But we can teach people to want more than they have, to be impatient with what they have been told is their lot. We can teach the skills of a scientific and technical culture and the cultural virtues of imagination. Now it will be said that no education system has ever taught people the virtues of discontent: mass education has always been about obedience training, about teaching children to follow the rules of life's hard game. This may be true but it will have to change. Never has there been a sharper contradiction between education's tendency to focus on obedience training and society's need for daring and imaginative individualists. The future is unlikely to belong to those whose education consists in rote learning, to those taught to value security as the highest value. The future will not turn out as either you or I expect; those best prepared for the future will be those whose education teaches them to welcome the challenge of the unexpected. The future belongs to the imaginative, the daring, the agile, the cosmopolitan, the unafraid. But then it always did.

Notes

1. The Past in the Present *David Cannadine*

1. K. Robbins, 'History, the Historical Association and the "National Past" ', *History*, LXVI (1981), 413–14.
2. D. Cannadine, 'The Context, Performance and Meaning of Ritual: the British Monarchy and the "Invention of Tradition", *c*1820–1977', in E.J. Hobsbawm and T. Ranger, (eds), *The Invention of Tradition* (Cambridge, 1983).
3. J. Walvin, *Victorian Values* (London, 1987); P. Kneller, 'Thatcher's flawed view of the past', *The Independent*, 13 April 1987, p. 16.
4. D. White, 'The Born-Again Museum', *New Society*, 1 May 1987, 10–12.
5. D. Cannadine, 'British History: Past, Present – and Future?', *Past and Present*, 116 (1987), 176.
6. G. Kitson Clark, 'A Hundred Years of History Teaching at Cambridge, 1873–1973', *Historical Journal*, XVI (1973), 535–53; R. Soffer, 'Nation, Duty, Character and Confidence: History at Oxford, 1850–1914', *Historical Journal*, XXX (1987), 77–104.
7. P. Darby, *Three Faces of Imperialism: British and American Approaches to Asia and Africa, 1870–1970* (1987), p. 23.
8. For one example of this, see J.H. Plumb, 'The Historian', in A.J.P. Taylor *et al.*, *Churchill: Four Faces and the Man* (Harmondsworth, 1969), pp. 119–24.
9. D. Cannadine, 'British Worthies', *London Review of Books*, 3–16 Dec. 1981, pp. 3–6.
10. For example, M. Creighton, *The English National Character* (London, 1896); A. Bryant, *The National Character* (London, 1934).
11. D.A. Low, *The Contraction of England* (Cambridge, 1984), pp. 10, 25–7.
12. Cannadine, 'British History', pp. 186–7.
13. For a powerful – but rather uninfluential – attack on the *Annales* school see B. Bailyn, 'Braudel's Geohistory – a reconsideration', *Journal of Economic History*, XI (1951), 277–82.
14. J.H. Hexter, *Reappraisals in History* (1961), pp. 194–5.
15. T. Zeldin, 'Ourselves, as We See Us', *Times Literary Supplement*, 31 Dec. 1982, pp. 1435–6.
16. T. Bender, 'Making History Whole Again', *New York Times Book Review*, 6 Oct. 1985, pp. 1, 42–3.
17. R.H.C. Davies, 'The Content of History', *History*, LXVI (1981), 367.

18. For two recent – and very differing – views on how this should be done, see W. Rees-Mogg, 'A grasp of the past is the key to understanding the present', *The Independent*, 21 July 1987, p. 14; N. Ascherson, 'Tell the children Wolfe won Quebec', *The Observer*, 26 July 1987, p. 7.

2. Britannia Overruled: the Shrinking of a World Power   *David Reynolds*

1. Cf. this comment by A.J.P. Taylor: 'The British did not relinquish their Empire by accident. They ceased to believe in it.' Quoted in Wm. Roger Louis, *Imperialism at Bay: The United States and the Decolonization of the British Empire* (Oxford, 1977), p. x.
2. See, for example, the works by Correlli Barnett, *The Collapse of British Power* (London, 1972), and *The Audit of War: The Illusion and Reality of Britain as a Great Nation* (London, 1986).
3. Colin McEvedy and Richard Jones, *Atlas of World Population History* (Harmondsworth, 1978), pp. 49, 81, 290.
4. D.K. Fieldhouse, *The Colonial Empires: A Comparative Survey from the Eighteenth Century* (London, 1982), p. 242.
5. Judith M. Brown, *Modern India: The Origins of an Asian Democracy* (Oxford, 1985), pp. 95–6, 188.
6. Curzon to Balfour, 31 March 1901, quoted in David Dilks, *Curzon in India* (London, 1969), Vol. I, p. 113.
7. Cf. D.A. Low, *The Contraction of England* (Cambridge, 1984), pp. 3–6.
8. On these crucial developments see John Gallagher, *The Decline, Revival and Fall of the British Empire*, ed. Anil Seal (Cambridge, 1982), pp. 138–9, 144.
9. T.O. Lloyd, *The British Empire, 1558–1983* (Oxford, 1984), p. 250; V.G. Kiernan, *European Empires from Conquest to Collapse, 1815–1960* (London, 1982), p. 80.
10. Nicholas Bethell, *The Palestine Triangle: The Struggle between the British, the Jews and the Arabs, 1935–48* (London, 1979), pp. 253–67; Thurston Clarke, *By Blood and Fire: The Attack on the King David Hotel* (New York, 1981).
11. Paul M. Kennedy, *The Rise and Fall of British Naval Mastery* (London, 1976), pp. 209, 285, 293–4.
12. Martin Middlebrook and Patrick Mahoney, *Battleship: The Loss of the Prince of Wales and the Repulse* (Harmondsworth, 1979).
13. House of Commons, *Debates*, 5th series, 30 July 1934, vol. 292, col. 2339.
14. For statistics in this and previous paragraph see Paul Bairoch, 'International Industrialization Levels from 1750 to 1980', *Journal of European Economic History*, 11 (Fall 1982), 296, 304.
15. I am extending here the analysis of imperial decline suggested in B.R. Tomlinson, 'The Contraction of England: National Decline and the Loss of Empire', *Journal of Imperial and Commonwealth History*, 11 (Oct. 1982), 58–72.

16. Paul M. Kennedy, *The Rise of the Anglo-German Antagonism, 1860–1914* (London, 1980), p. 467.

17. For a recent discussion of the 'thirty years war' theory see P.M.H. Bell, *The Origins of the Second World War in Europe* (London, 1986).

18. B.R. Mitchell, with Phyllis Deane, *Abstract of British Historical Statistics* (Cambridge, 1962), p. 399.

19. *The Times*, 17 Nov. 1964, p. 6, quoting Wilson's Guildhall speech the previous evening.

20. Sir Orme Sargent, minute, 1 Oct. 1945, Foreign Office General Political Correspondence, FO 371/44557, AN 2560/22/45 (Public Record Office, London). Crown copyright documents in the PRO are quoted by permission of the Controller of HM Stationery Office.

21. Foreign Office memo, 21 Mar. 1944, 'The Essentials of an American Policy', FO 371/38523, AN 1538/16/45 (PRO).

22. Labour Party, National Executive Committee, *European Unity* (London, 1950), p. 4. On British policy and attitudes see John W. Young, *Britain, France and the Unity of Europe, 1945–1951* (Leicester, 1984); Jeremy Moon, *European Integration in British Politics, 1950–1963: A Study of Issue Change* (Aldershot, 1985).

23. For this argument see Sidney Pollard, *The Wasting of the British Economy: British Economic Policy, 1945 to the Present* (London, 1982); Malcolm Chalmers, *Paying for Defence: Military Spending and British Decline* (London, 1985).

3. The Decline of Britain?   *Richard Overy*

1. The figures for average incomes are in real terms, that is adjusted for price changes. The unadjusted figures for British Gross National Product show the sheer scale of economic growth over the century:

(£m)			
1900	2,032	1950	21,733
1910	2,328	1960	28,214
1920	4,160	1970	37,775
1930	4,905	1980	225,560
1940	6,739		

The great increase between 1940 and 1980 is a result of high levels of inflation. But even adjusted for price changes the economy grew 75 per cent between 1950 and 1970, and a further 20 per cent between 1970 and 1979. For statistics on the British economy see B.R. Mitchell, *European Historical Statistics 1850–1970* (London, 1978) and M.H. Peston, *The British Economy* (Oxford, 1982).

2. C.H. Saxelby (ed.), *Bolton Survey* (Bolton, 1953), pp. 86–101.

3. K. Richardson, *Twentieth Century Coventry* (London, 1972); D. Thomas and T. Donnelly, *The Motor Car Industry in Coventry since the 1890s* (London, 1985).

4. D. Aldcroft, *The British Economy between the Wars* (Oxford, 1983);

B.W. Alford, *Depression and Recovery? British Economic Growth 1918–1939* (London, 1972); N. Buxton, D. Aldcroft (eds), *British Industry between the Wars* (London, 1979).

5. S. Pollard, *The Development of the British Economy 1914–1967* (2nd edn.), (London, 1969), p. 290; D. Aldcroft, *The Inter-War Economy: Britain 1919–1939* (London, 1970), pp. 362–7. On increases in consumer expenditure, and the changing pattern of spending, see R. Stone and D.A. Rowe, *The Measurement of Consumers' Expenditure and Behaviour in the United Kingdom 1920–1938* (Cambridge, 1966).

6. J. Jeffreys, *Retail Trading in Britain 1850–1950* (Cambridge, 1954); P. Mathias, *Retailing Revolution* (London, 1967).

7. R.J. Overy, *William Morris, Viscount Nuffield* (London, 1976).

8. See the discussion of the electronics industry in P. Pagnamenta and R.J. Overy, *All Our Working Lives* (London, 1984).

9. On this period see G. Turner, *Business in Britain* (London, 1969); P.J. Dunnett, *The Decline of the British Motor Industry 1945–1979* (London, 1980); I. Berkovitch, *Coal on the Switchback* (London, 1977); D.W. Heal, *The Steel Industry in Post-War Britain* (Newton Abbot, 1974); S. Pollard, *The Wasting of the British Economy* (London, 1982).

10. F. Engledow and L. Amey, *Britain's Future in Farming* (Berkhamsted, 1980).

11. A. Peacock and J. Wiseman, *The Growth of Public Expenditure in the United Kingdom* (London, 1967), pp. 164–5. Expenditure developed as follows (at constant 1900 prices):

(£m)			
1895	172.3	1938	851.2
1910	263.6	1947	1,243.0
1920	565.3	1955	1,309.0
1930	601.8		

As a percentage of GNP government expenditure rose from 8.95 per cent in 1890 to 49 per cent in 1974.

12. J. Leruez, *Economic Planning & Politics in Britain* (London, 1975); J.C. Dow, *The Management of the British Economy 1945–1960* (Cambridge, 1965). On the effects of the two wars see A.S. Milward, *The Economic Effects of the Two World Wars on Britain* (London, 1970).

13. L. Hannah and J.A. Kay, *Concentration in Modern Industry* (London, 1977); L. Hannah, *The Rise of the Corporate Economy* (London, 1976). The share of the 100 largest firms in manufacturing net output increased as follows:

1909	15%	1953	26%
1919	17	1958	33
1939	23	1968	42

14. For recent literature on this theme see M.J. Wiener, *English Culture and the Decline of the Industrial Spirit* (Cambridge, 1981); K. Williams, J. Williams and D. Thomas, *Why are the British so bad at manufacturing?* (London, 1983); M.W. Kirby, *The Decline of British Economic Power since 1870* (London, 1981).

4. The New Jerusalem *John Stevenson*

1. *Picture Post*, 4 Jan. 1941.
2. Samuel Smiles, *Self-Help*, reprint edition (London, 1968), pp. 11–14.
3. W. Booth, *In Darkest England and the Way Out*, reprint edn (London, 1970), pp. 78–9.
4. *The Memoirs of the Rt. Hon. The Earl of Woolton* (London, 1959), p. 6.
5. For some of the writings of Booth and Rowntree, as well as other social investigators, see P. Keating, *Into Unknown England, 1866–1913* (London, 1976) and J. Stevenson, *Social Conditions in Britain between the Wars* (Harmondsworth, 1977).
6. For an inside account of slum life, see Helen Forrester, *Twopence to Cross the Mersey* (London, 1974).
7. See E. Howard, *Garden Cities of Tomorrow* (London, 1946).
8. M. Swenarton, *Homes Fit for Heroes* (London, 1981).
9. For a description of the Liverpool estates, see D. Caradog Jones (ed.), *The Social Survey of Merseyside* (Liverpool and London, 1934).
10. See B.S. Rowntree, *Poverty and Progress* (London, 1941) for York and E.D. Simon, *How to Abolish the Slums* (London, 1929), pp. 99–101.
11. E.D. Simon and J. Inman, *The Rebuilding of Manchester* (London, 1935), p. 81.
12. For the wartime developments see P. Addison, *The Road to 1945* (London, 1975), pp. 174–8 and J.B. Cullingworth, *Town and Country Planning in England and Wales* (London, 1967), pp. 27–31.
13. K. Richardson, *Twentieth-Century Coventry* (Coventry, 1972), pp. 277–309.
14. See F.J. Osborn and A. Whittick, *New Towns: the Origins, Achievements, and Progress* (London, 1977).
15. J. Burnett, *A Social History of Housing, 1815–1970* (London, 1980), pp. 276–95.
16. M. Young and P. Willmott, *Family and Kinship in East London* (London, 1957). See also R. Hoggart, *The Uses of Literacy* (London, 1957), especially ch. 2.
17. B.S. Rowntree and G.R. Lavers, *English Life and Leisure: a Social Study* (London, 1951) which opens with the proverb 'Life is not a vessel to be drained, but a cup to be filled'.
18. Burnett, op. cit., pp. 288–9.

5. A Woman's Place *Pat Thane*

1. Lee Holcombe, *Victorian Ladies at Work: Middle-Class Working Women in England and Wales, 1850–1914* (Newton Abbot, 1973).
2. Margery Spring-Rice, *Working-Class Wives* (London, 1981), p. 36.
3. Michael Anderson, 'The Emergence of the Modern Life-cycle in Britain', *Social History*, 10, No. 1.
4. P. Branca, *Silent Sisterhood* (London, 1975).

5. Elizabeth Roberts, *A Woman's Place. An Oral History of Working-class Women* (Oxford, 1984); Melanie Tebbutt, *Making Ends Meet. Pawnbroking and Working-Class Credit* (Leicester, 1983).
6. Clementina Black (ed.), *Married Women's Work* (London, 1983), p. 10.
7. Quoted in Jane Mackay and Pat Thane, 'The Englishwoman' in R. Colls and P. Dodd, *Englishness. Politics and Culture 1880–1920* (London, 1986).
8. F. Prochaska, *Women and Philanthropy in 19th Century England* (Oxford, 1980).
9. *Daily Telegraph*, 27 Mar. 1888; 3 Apr. 1988.
10. See O.R. McGregor, *Divorce in England* (London, 1953) and G.B. Shaw, *Preface to Getting Married* (London, 1906).
11. A. Marwick, *The Deluge. A Social History of World War One* (Harmondsworth, 1965).
12. J.M. Winter, *The Great War and the British People* (London, 1985), p. 193.
13. P. Summerfield, *Women Workers in the Second World War* (London, 1984).
14. Denise Riley, *War in the Nursery* (London, 1983).
15. William Crofts, 'The Attlee Government's pursuit of Women', *History Today*, Aug. 1986, pp. 29–39.
16. D.W. Winnicott, *The Child, the Family and the Outside World* (Harmondsworth, 1964), p. 120.
17. See Martha Vicinus, *Independent Women. Work and Community for Single Women 1850–1930* (London, 1984).

6. In Place of Fear   *Adrian Wooldridge*

1. Margaret Thatcher, *Let our Children Grow Tall. Selected Speeches 1975–1977* (London, 1977), p. 1.
2. Asa Briggs, 'The Welfare State in Historical Perspective', *The Collected Essays of Asa Briggs Volume Two. Images, Problems, Standpoints, Forecasts* (Brighton, 1985), p. 183.
3. Bentley B. Gilbert, *The Evolution of National Insurance in Great Britain. The Origins of the Welfare State* (London, 1966), p. 9.
4. See Gilbert, *Evolution of National Insurance* and G.R. Searle, *The Quest for National Efficiency. A Study in British Politics and Political Thought 1899–1914* (Oxford, 1971).
5. Gilbert, *Evolution of National Insurance*, p. 61.
6. *The Child. A Monthly Journal Devoted to Child Welfare* (ed. T.N. Kelynack), 1, No. 1 (Oct. 1910), p. 1.
7. See Michael Freeden, *The New Liberalism. An Ideology of Social Reform* (Oxford, 1978).
8. A. Milner, Introduction to A. Toynbee, *Lectures on the Industrial Revolution* (London, 1923), p. xxv.
9. See Melvin Richter, *The Politics of Conscience. T.H. Green and His Age* (London, 1964), esp. pp. 267–92.

10. Gilbert, *Evolution of National Insurance*, pp. 41–2. José Harris, *William Beveridge. A Biography* (Oxford, 1977), pp. 44–63.
11. Quoted in Stefan Collini, *Liberalism and Sociology. L.T. Hobhouse and Political Argument in England 1880–1914* (Cambridge, 1979), p. 139 fn.
12. Norman and Jean MacKenzie, *The First Fabians* (London, 1977), p. 59. See also A.M. McBriar, *Fabian Socialism and English Politics 1884–1918* (Cambridge, 1962), esp. pp. 146–62.
13. See, for example, Beatrice Webb, *Our Partnership* (London, 1948), pp. 194–5.
14. Douglas E. Ashford, *The Emergence of the Welfare States* (Oxford, 1986), pp. 106–85.
15. See Paul Addison, *The Road to 1945. British Politics and the Second World War* (London, 1975), pp. 23–52.
16. Quoted in Briggs, 'The Welfare State in Historical Perspective', p. 182.
17. J.M. Winter and D.M. Joslin (eds), *R.H. Tawney's Commonplace Book* (Cambridge, 1972), pp. 26–7. Quoted in Addison, *The Road to 1945*, p. 212.
18. Harris, *Beveridge*, pp. 402–5.
19. Douglas Jay, *The Socialist Case* (Harmondsworth, 1947), p. 258.
20. Ashford, *Emergence of the Welfare States*, p. 312. See Titmuss's essay 'Welfare "Rights", Law and Discretion', *Political Quarterly*, 42, No. 2 (April–June 1971), 113–32.
21. Ashford, *Emergence of the Welfare States*, pp. 273–4, 277–9.
22. See Rudolf Klein, *The Politics of the National Health Service* (London, 1983).
23. See Malcolm Wicks, *A Future for All. Do We Need a Welfare State?* (Harmondsworth, 1987), pp. 35–9.
24. R.H. Tawney, *Equality* (1st pub. 1931, 1964 edn with an introduction by Richard Titmuss), p. 149.
25. Department of Health and Social Security, 'Inequalities in Health: report of a research working group' (1980). Also available as Peter Townsend and Nick Davidson (eds), *Inequalities in Health: the Black Report* (Harmondsworth, 1982).
26. See A.H. Halsey, A.F. Heath and J.M. Ridge, *Origins and Destinations: Family, Class and Education in Modern Britain* (Oxford, 1980). This research is conveniently summarised in Anthony Heath, 'Class in the Classroom', *New Society*, 17 July 1987, pp. 13–14. See also Julian Le Grand, *The Strategy of Equality. Redistribution and the Social Services* (London, 1982), pp. 54–81.
27. See Wicks, *A Future for All*, pp. 105–9.
28. Sir William Beveridge, *Social Insurance and Allied Services*, Cmnd 6404 (HMSO, 1942), para. 270.
29. See, for example, R. Bacon and W.A. Eltis, *Britain's Economic Problem. Too Few Producers* (London, 1978).
30. Wicks, *A Future for All*, p. 32.
31. Barbara Wootton in Philip Bean and Stewart MacPherson (eds), *Approaches to Welfare* (London, 1983), p. 286.
32. *The Government's Expenditure Plans 1985/6–1987/8* Cmnd 9428–11 (HMSO, 1985) Table 2.6.

7. Mass Media, Mass Democracy   *Paddy Scannell*

1. Women were given equal voting rights with men in 1928. The long political struggle to establish the old radical cry of 'one man one vote' goes back to the English civil war in the mid seventeenth century. The history of women's struggle for equal political rights with men is separate from this, and is well described by Sheila Rowbotham, *Hidden from History* (London, 1973).
2. The essays in G. McLennan, D. Held and S. Hall (eds), *State and Society in Contemporary Britain* (Cambridge, 1984) offer useful accounts of many aspects of the development of modern British politics.
3. Susan Briggs, *Those Radio Times* (London, 1981) is a profusely illustrated account of the impact of broadcasting on ordinary life before the war.
4. The early history of the radio set is well illustrated and told by Jonathan Hill, *The Cat's Whisker* (London, 1978).
5. Shaun Moores describes people's responses to the arrival of the radio in the living room before the war in ' "The box on the dresser": memories of early radio and everyday life', *Media Culture & Society*, 10 (1988), no. 1.
6. See Simon Frith, 'The pleasures of the hearth; the making of BBC light entertainment', *Formations of Pleasure* (London, 1983).
7. Quoted in *Radio Times*, 12 Oct. 1923.
8. Hilda Jennings and Winifred Gill, *Broadcasting and Everyday Life* (London, 1939).
9. John Reith, *Broadcast Over Britain* (London, 1924), pp. 18–19.
10. Two useful accounts of this history may be found in Grace Wyndham Goldie, *Facing the Nation. Television and Politics, 1936–1976* (London, 1977) and Philip Schlesinger, *Putting 'reality' together: BBC news* (London, 1978).
11. The best account of the role of the BBC in the general strike is in Asa Briggs, 'The Birth of Broadcasting', *The History of Broadcasting in the United Kingdom* (Oxford, 1961), vol. 1, pp. 360–84.
12. On Munich see Paddy Scannell, 'Broadcasting and Foreign Affairs, 1935–1939', *Media Culture & Society*, 6 (1984), no. 1. On Suez see Asa Briggs, *Governing the BBC* (London, 1979), pp. 209–17 and Goldie, *Facing the Nation*, pp. 175–87. On the Falklands War see Robert Harris, *Gotcha! The Media, the Government and the Falklands Crisis* (London, 1983).
13. *BBC Yearbook* (London, 1928), p. 85.
14. For a fuller account of this process see David Cardiff and Paddy Scannell, 'Broadcasting and national unity', in J. Curran, A. Smith and P. Wingate (eds), *Impacts and Influences: Essays on Media Power in the 20th Century* (London, 1987).
15. This argument is based on the writings of Raymond Williams, especially *The Long Revolution* (Harmondsworth, 1965).
16. A fuller account of this programme and those dealing with unemploy-

ment and housing in the 1930s can be found in Paddy Scannell, ' "The stuff of radio". Developments in radio features and documentaries before the war', in J. Corner (ed.), *Documentary and the Mass Media* (London, 1986).

17. For an excellent recent study of how people in families watch television, see David Morley, *Family Television: Cultural Power and Domestic Leisure* (London, 1986).
18. For a fuller discussion of how broadcasting adapts its services to the routines of everyday life see Paddy Scannell, '*Radio Times*: the temporal arrangements of broadcasting in the modern world', in P. Drummond (ed.), *Television and its Audience: International Research Perspectives* (London, 1988).
19. Two good books on British TV soap operas are Richard Dyer *et al.* (eds), *Coronation Street* (London, 1981), and Dorothy Hobson, *Crossroads. The Drama of a Soap Opera* (London, 1982).
20. *Guardian*, 4 Jan. 1982, quoted in John Tulloch and Manuel Alvarado, *Dr Who. The Unfolding Text* (London, 1983).
21. For a full discussion of differing versions of democracy, past and present, and some possible future developments, see David Held, *Models of Democracy* (Cambridge, 1987).
22. I have in mind here the contrast between representative and participatory democracy discussed in ibid., pp. 259–61.

8. People and Power   *Kenneth O. Morgan*

1. For a good treatment of the franchise question, see Martin Pugh, *The Making of Modern British Politics, 1867–1939* (Oxford, 1982). More detailed discussions occur in Neal Blewett, 'The Franchise in the United Kingdom, 1885–1918', *Past and Present* (Dec. 1965) and H.C.G. Matthew, R.I. McKibbin and J.A. Kay, 'The Franchise Factor in the Rise of the Labour Party', *English Historical Review* (Oct. 1976). The latter article is criticised by Michael Hart, 'The Liberals, the War and the Franchise', *EHR* (Oct. 1982).
2. On these matters, see Eric Hobsbawm, *Labouring Men* (London, 1986) and *Worlds of Labour* (London, 1984), for a Marxist perspective. For a critique, see Henry Pelling, 'The Concept of the Labour Aristocracy' in *Popular Politics and Society in late Victorian Britain* (London, 1968). William Ashworth, *An Economic History of England, 1870–1939* (London, 1960) is valuable for background.
3. See Henry Pelling, *Origins of the Labour Party, 1880–1900* (London, 1954), E.H. Phelps Brown, *The Origins of Trade Union Power* (Oxford, 1983); and H. Clegg, A. Fox and A.F. Thompson, *A History of British Trade Unions since 1889*, vol. I (Oxford, 1964), chs 2–4.
4. For Henderson, see the relevant chapter in Kenneth O. Morgan, *Labour People* (Oxford, 1987) and R.I. McKibbin, *The Evolution of the Labour Party, 1910–1924* (Oxford, 1974).

5. For the Fabians, see A.M. McBriar, *Fabian Socialism and English Politics, 1884–1918* (Cambridge, 1963); Lisanne Radice, *Beatrice and Sidney Webb: Fabian Socialists* (London, 1984); and Patricia Pugh, *Educate, Organize: 100 Years of Fabian Socialism* (London, 1984).

6. The outstanding work on the ILP is David Howell, *British Workers and the Independent Labour Party, 1888–1906* (Manchester, 1983).

7. See David Marquand, *Ramsay MacDonald* (London, 1977); and Kenneth O. Morgan, *Keir Hardie, Radical and Socialist* (Oxford, 1984).

8. An excellent guide here is Roy Gregory, *The Miners and British Politics, 1906–14* (London, 1968).

9. See Kenneth O. Morgan, *The Age of Lloyd George* (Oxford, 1978); and Bruce K. Murray, *The People's Budget* (Oxford, 1980). Bentley Brinkerhoff Gilbert, *David Lloyd George: the Architect of Change, 1863–1912* (London, 1987) takes a different view.

10. J.M. Winter, *Socialism and the Challenge of War* (London and Boston, 1974) and Walter Kendall, *The Revolutionary Movement in Great Britain, 1900–1921* (London, 1969) offer contrasting interpretations. Also relevant is James Hinton, *The First Shop Stewards' Movement* (London, 1973), a thesis powerfully criticised by Ian McLean, 'The Ministry of Munitions, The Clyde Workers Committee and the suppression of "Forward" ', *Scottish Journal of Labour History* (Dec. 1972).

11. See particularly, G.A. Phillips, *The General Strike* (London, 1976) and Alan Bullock, *The Life and Times of Ernest Bevin*, vol. 1 (London, 1960). For a colourful account of developments in one coalfield, see Hywel Francis and David Smith, *The Fed* (London, 1980).

12. For the 1931 crisis, see Robert Skidelsky, *Politicians and the Slump* (London, 1968), Marquand, *MacDonald*, and Bullock, *Bevin*, vol. 1. The aftermath is well covered in Ben Pimlott, *Labour and the Left in the 1930s* (Cambridge, 1977).

13. Splendid discussions appear in Elizabeth Durbin, *New Jerusalems* (London, 1985) and Ben Pimlott, *Hugh Dalton* (London, 1985). Two contemporary works still well worth reading are Douglas Jay, *The Socialist Case* (London, 1937), to be read in conjunction with his later memoirs, *Change and Fortune* (London, 1980), and Evan Durbin, *The Politics of Democratic Socialism* (London, 1940).

14. See Bernard Donoughue and G.W. Jones, *Herbert Morrison: Portrait of a Politician* (London, 1973).

15. For Wales and Scotland, see Kenneth O. Morgan, *Rebirth of a Nation: Wales 1880–1980* (Oxford, 1981); Christopher Harvie, *No Gods and Precious Few Heroes: Scotland 1914–1980* (London, 1981); and David Howell, *A Lost Left* (Manchester, 1986).

16. The outstanding work on Labour and the Second World War is Paul Addison, *The Road to 1945* (London, 1975). Angus Calder, *The People's War* (London, 1971) is lively. Also see Pimlott, *Hugh Dalton*, and Kenneth Harris, *Attlee* (London, 1982).

17. The Attlee government is variously covered in Kenneth O. Morgan,

Labour in Power, 1945–1951 (Oxford, 1984); Henry Pelling, *The Labour Governments of 1945–51* (London, 1984); Michael Sissons and Philip French (eds), *The Age of Austerity, 1945–1951* (Oxford, 1986); and David Howell, *British Social Democracy* (London, 1980). Also see John Campbell, *Nye Bevan* (London, 1987).

18. The troubles of the 1950s are treated, from rival perspectives, in Kenneth O. Morgan, *Labour People*; John Campbell, *Nye Bevan*; Philip Williams, *Hugh Gaitskell* (London, 1979); and Stephen Haseler, *The Gaitskellites* (Oxford, 1969). A fascinating, if flawed, first-hand source is Janet Morgan (ed.), *The Backbench Diaries of Richard Crossman* (London, 1981).

19. There is no adequate account of the Wilson government to date. Wilson's own memoirs, *The Labour Government, 1964–70: a personal memoir* (London, 1971) are very suspect. More useful is James Callaghan, *Time and Chance* (London, 1987). A fascinating essay is Alec Cairncross, 'The 1967 Devaluation of Sterling' in A. Cairncross and B. Eichengreen, *Sterling in Decline* (Oxford, 1983). Also see Tony Benn, *Out of the Wilderness: Diaries, 1963–67* (London, 1987).

20. There is much scrappy or journalistic literature on this theme. Most useful, perhaps, are H.M. Drucker, *Doctrine and Ethos in the Labour Party* (London, 1979); David Kogan and Maurice Kogan, *The Battle for the Labour Party* (London, 1982); Dennis Kavanagh (ed.), *The Politics of the Labour Party* (London, 1982); Paul Whiteley, *The Labour Party in Crisis* (London, 1983); and Martin Adeney and John Lloyd, *The Miners' Strike, 1984–5* (London, 1986).

21. See Kenneth O. Morgan, 'The Rise and Fall of Public Ownership in Great Britain', in J.M.W. Bean (ed.), *The Political Culture of Modern Britain* (London, 1987).

9. The Myth of Consensus   *Ben Pimlott*

1. Paul Addison, *The Road to 1945: British Politics and the Second World War* (London, 1977), p. 14.
2. See C. Barnett, *The Audit of War* (London, 1987).
3. Addison, op. cit., p. 14.
4. M. Macmillan, *The Middle Way: A Study of the Problem of Economic and Social Progress in a Free and Democratic Society* (London, 1938).
5. D. Kavanagh, *Thatcherism and British Politics: The End of Consensus?* (Oxford, 1987), p. 46.
6. S.H. Beer, *Britain against Itself: The Political Contradictions of Collectivism* (London, 1982), p. 9.

10. The Dark Strangers   *Michael Gilkes*

1. Terry Eagleton, *Exiles and Emigrés* (London, 1970), p. 9.
2. Frank Delaney, *The Celts* (London, 1986), p. 224.

3. W. Cunningham, *Alien Immigrants to England* (London, 1897), p. 270.
4. Ibid., p. 77.
5. *Hansard*, 45H⅛145⅜717, 2 May 1905.
6. Edward Kamau Brathwaite's trilogy, *The Arrivants* (Oxford, 1981) is a historically-based, poetic evocation of the migrations of the Akhan peoples of Africa and the resultant Black Diaspora.
7. See Amos A. Ford, *Telling the Truth* (Karia Press, 1985). A detailed and interesting account of the blatant racial prejudice that bedevilled this exercise.
8. Cited in P. Gordon and F. King, *British Immigration Control: a Brief Guide* (London, 1985), p. 3. This charts the development of British Immigration Law, pointing out its racial bias.
9. Walter Trott, *Royal Commission on Alien Immigration* (London, 1903), vol. II, p. 99.
10. See Paul Foot, *Immigration and Race in British Politics* (Harmondsworth, 1965), p. 36.
11. See N. Deakin, *Colour and the British Electorate* (London, 1965), p. 91.
12. Samuel Smiles, *Self-Help* (London, 1859), a Victorian best-seller extolling the virtues of patience, fortitude and industry.
13. Charles Rolleston, *New Liberal Review* (March 1904), p. 18.
14. *Sunday Times*, 28 June 1987, p. 53.
15. V.S. Naipaul, *Miguel Street* (London, 1959), p. 29.
16. Sam Selvon, *The Lonely Londoners* (London, 1956), p. 121.
17. *Daily Advertiser*, No. 13, 13 Dec. 1744.
18. David Dabydeen, *Hogarth's Blacks* (Warwick, 1985), pp. 21–9. An excellent study of the pervasive, but long-ignored, presence of blacks in the art (and therefore the life) of eighteenth-century Britain.
19. Nigel File and Chris Power, *Black Settlers in Britain: 1555–1958* (London, 1981), pp. 2–4.
20. *The Gentleman's Magazine*, vol. 34 (1764), p. 493.
21. File and Power, *Black Settlers*, pp. 60–4.
22. Ibid.
23. Derek Walcott, *The Gulf* (London, 1972), p. 51.
24. Sevlon, *Lonely Londoners*, pp. 72–3.
25. File and Power, *Black Settlers*, p. 87.
26. Cited in Gordon and King, *British Immigration*, p. 5.
27. Ibid., p. 6.
28. Ibid., p. 22.
29. V.S. Naipaul, *The Enigma of Arrival* (London, 1986), p. 301.

11. A Prosperous People   *Leslie Hannah*

1. Paul Thompson, *The Voice of the Past: oral history* (Oxford, 1978).
2. Leslie Hannah, *Inventing Retirement: the development of occupational pensions in Britain* (Cambridge, 1986).

3. R.C.O. Matthews, C.H. Feinstein and J.C. Odling-Smee, *British Economic Growth, 1856–1973* (Oxford, 1982).
4. M. Bienefeld, *Working House in British Industry: an economic history* (London, 1972).
5. A.B. Atkinson, *Unequal Shares: wealth in Britain*, revised edn (Harmondsworth, 1974).
6. Derek H. Aldcroft and Peter Fearon (eds), *Economic Growth in Twentieth-Century Britain* (London, 1969).
7. Leslie Hannah, *Electricity before Nationalisation: a study of the development of the electricity supply industry in Britain to 1948* (London, 1979).
8. Paul Johnson, *Saving and Spending: the working class economy in Britain 1870–1939* (Oxford, 1985).
9. G.C. Allen, *The British Disease: a short essay on the nature and causes of the nation's lagging wealth*, 2nd edn, Hobart Paper: 67 (London, 1979).
10. Edward F. Denison, *Why Growth Rates Differ: Post war experience in 9 western countries* (Washington DC, 1982).
11. Angus Maddison, *Phases of Capitalist Development* (Oxford; New York, 1982).
12. Margaret Ackrill, *Manufacturing Industry since 1870* (Oxford, 1987).

Notes on Contributors

DAVID CANNADINE is Professor of History at Columbia University. He is the author of *Lords and Landlords: The Aristocracy and the Towns, 1774–1967* (1980) and *The Pleasures of the Past* (1988). He is the editor or co-editor of *Patricians, Power and Politics in Nineteenth Century Towns* (1982), *Exploring the Urban Past: essays in Urban History by H.J. Dyos* (1982), and *Rituals of Royalty: Power and Ceremonial in Traditional Societies* (1987). He has published essays and articles on the social, political, economic and cultural history of modern Britain, and he is a regular contributor to the *New York Review of Books* and other journals. He is at present working on a two-volume history of the aristocracy in modern Britain.

MICHAEL GILKES, born in Guyana, is a senior lecturer in English at the University of the West Indies, Barbados. He has a doctorate in American and English Studies from the University of Kent, and has taught at the universities of Guyana, Kent and Warwick, where he was visiting Leverhulme Fellow at the Centre for Caribbean Studies in 1986/7. His publications include *Wilson Harris and the Caribbean Novel* (1975), *The West Indian Novel* (1981) and two plays: *Couvade* (1974) and *In Transit* (1980). He has devised and produced educational radio and TV programmes on Caribbean writers and their work, and is currently at work on a handbook ('The Living Text'), a new play and a critical work.

LESLIE HANNAH has taught at the universities of Essex, Oxford, Cambridge, Harvard and Hitotsubashi, Tokyo. He is currently Professor of Business History at the London School of Economics. His books include *The Rise of the Corporate Economy, Electricity before Nationalisation, Engineers, Managers and Politicians* and *Inventing Retirement*. He is currently working on a study of the causes of Britain's long-run economic decline and on pensions policy.

MICHAEL IGNATIEFF is a Harvard-educated historian, whose books include *A Just Measure of Pain, The Needs of Strangers* and *The Russian Album*. He is the presenter of BBC's *Thinking Aloud*.

KENNETH O. MORGAN has been Fellow in Modern History and Politics at The Queen's College, Oxford, since 1966 and a Fellow of the British Academy since 1983. His many books include *Wales in British Politics* (1963), *The Age of Lloyd George* (1971), *Lloyd George* (1974), *Keir Hardie, Radical and Socialist* (1975), *Consensus and Disunity* (1979), *Rebirth of a Nation: Wales 1880–1980* (1981), (ed.) *The Oxford Illustrated History of Britain* (1984), *Labour in Power, 1945–51* (1984) and *Labour People* (1987). He has edited *The Welsh History Review* since 1961. He is currently writing a history of Britain since the Second World War.

RICHARD OVERY is a lecturer in modern history at King's College, London. He has written extensively on modern German and British history. His books include *William Morris, Viscount Nuffield* and *The Air War 1939–1945*. He is currently writing a history of the Nazi economy, and a history of Europe since 1945. He is also working on a series of television documentaries on the origins of the Second World War to mark its fiftieth anniversary, and is co-author of the accompanying book *Road to War*.

BEN PIMLOTT is Professor of Politics at Birkbeck College, University of London. He is the author of *Labour and the Left in the 1930s* and *Hugh Dalton*, which won the Whitbread Biography Award, and editor of the Dalton diaries. He is a political columnist on the *New Statesman* and *The Times* and reviews regularly for the *Observer*.

DAVID REYNOLDS is Fellow and Director of Studies at Christ's College, Cambridge, and University Assistant Lecturer in the History of International Relations. He has taught and researched extensively in the USA, including three periods as a visiting fellow at Harvard University. He is the author of *The Creation of the Anglo-American Alliance, 1937–41* (1981), which was awarded the Bernath Prize in the USA, and of *An Ocean Apart: The Relationship between Britain and America in the Twentieth Century* (1988), co-author David Dimbleby, which accompanied the TV series for which Dr Reynolds was historical consultant.

PADDY SCANNELL is a senior lecturer in the Department of Media Studies at the Polytechnic of Central London. He has written many articles on broadcast history and is presently writing a social history of British broadcasting. He is one of the founding editors of *Media Culture and Society*, a quarterly international journal that explores the political, social and cultural effects of the media in modern societies.

LESLEY SMITH studied history at the University of St Andrews and Brasenose College, Oxford. She lectured in Vancouver, taught in Edinburgh and worked for the civil service in London before joining London Weekend Television where she first researched and latterly produced the sixty programmes in the *Making of Britain* series. Her books include *The General Crisis of the Seventeenth Century* (with Geoffrey Parker), and she has edited the first four volumes in the *Making of Britain* series.

JOHN STEVENSON was educated at Boteler Grammar School, Warrington, and Worcester College, Oxford. After teaching at Oriel College, Oxford, for five years, he is now reader in History at the University of Sheffield. His research interests have been largely concentrated on social history and popular movements in Britain from the eighteenth century onwards. He has published *Social Conditions in Britain between the Wars* (1977), *The Slump: Politics and Society in the Depression*, with Chris Cook (1984). He is currently working on a study of the life and times of Wiliam Cobbett and a major new social history of Britain.

PAT THANE teaches at Goldsmith's College, University of London. She has written widely on the history of social welfare since the late nineteenth century and on other aspects of modern social history. Her publications include *The Foundations of the Welfare State* (1982) and *Essays in Social History*, ed. with A. Sutcliffe (1986).

ADRIAN WOOLDRIDGE read history at Balliol College, Oxford. In 1980 he was elected to a Prize Fellowship at All Souls College, Oxford. He spent 1984–5 as a Harkness Fellow at the University of California, Berkeley. *Psychology, Intelligence and Merit*, an expanded version of his DPhil thesis, will be published in 1988. He has several articles forthcoming in academic journals and is a frequent contributor to the *Times Literary Supplement*. His main interests lie in intellectual history, in the history of education and in social stratification.

Index